Slavoj Žižek

VIOLENCE

Slavoj Žižek is a senior researcher at the Institute of Sociology, University of Ljubljana, Slovenia, and has been a visiting professor at Columbia University, Princeton, and The New School. He is the author of more than thirty books and is the subject of the documentary *Žižek*. His own critically acclaimed documentary, *The Pervert's Guide to Cinema*, was the subject of a film retrospective in 2007 at the Museum of Modern Art.

Slavoj Žižek

VIOLENCE

Slavoj Žižek is a senior researcher at the Institute of Sociology, University of Ljubljana, Slovenia, and has been a visiting professor at Columbia University, Princeton, and the New School for Social Research, and more than a dozen other universities throughout the world. Among his many books are *The Sublime Object of Ideology*, *For They Know Not What They Do*, and *The Ticklish Subject*.

VIOLENCE

SIX SIDEWAYS REFLECTIONS

Slavoj Žižek

BIG IDEAS/SMALL BOOKS

PICADOR

New York

www.picadorusa.com

Picador® is a U.S. registered trademark and is used by St. Martin's Press under license from Pan Books Limited.

For information on Picador Reading Group Guides, please contact Picador.
E-mail: readinggroupguides@picadorusa.com

The poem "He Wishes for Cloths of Heaven" by W. B. Yeats is reprinted by permission of A P Watt Ltd on behalf of Gráinne. Yeats.

The poem "The Interrogation of the Good" (Vehör der Guten) by Bertolt Brecht is reprinted by permission from Bertolt Brecht, Werke. GroBe kommentierte Berliner und Frankfurter Ausgabe, Band 14: Gedichte 4, © Suhrkamp Verlag Frankfurt am Main 1993. English translation copyright © 2008 by Slavoj Žižek.

ISBN-13: 978-0-312-42718-4
ISBN-10: 0-312-42718-2

Originally published in Great Britain by Profile Books Ltd.
First Picador Edition: August 2008

D   22

CONTENTS

VIOLENCE

Introduction

THE TYRANT'S BLOODY ROBE

There is an old story about a worker suspected of stealing: every evening, as he leaves the factory, the wheelbarrow he rolls in front of him is carefully inspected. The guards can find nothing. It is always empty. Finally, the penny drops: what the worker is stealing are the wheelbarrows themselves . . .

If there is a unifying thesis that runs through the bric-a-brac of reflections on violence that follow, it is that a similar paradox holds true for violence. At the forefront of our minds, the obvious signals of violence are acts of crime and terror, civil unrest, international conflict. But we should learn to step back, to disentangle ourselves from the fascinating lure of this directly visible "subjective" violence, violence performed by a clearly identifiable agent. We need to perceive the contours of the background which generates such outbursts. A step back enables us to identify a violence that sustains our very efforts to fight violence and to promote tolerance.

This is the starting point, perhaps even the axiom, of the present book: subjective violence is just the most visible portion of a triumvirate that also includes two objective kinds of violence. First, there is a "symbolic" violence embodied in language and its forms, what Heidegger would call "our house of being." As we shall see later, this violence is not only at work in the obvious–and extensively studied–cases of incitement and of the relations of social domination reproduced in our habitual speech forms: there is a more fundamental form of violence still that pertains to language as such, to its imposition of a certain universe of meaning. Second, there is what I call "systemic" violence, or the often catastrophic consequences of the smooth functioning of our economic and political systems.

The catch is that subjective and objective violence cannot be perceived from the same standpoint: subjective violence is experienced as such against the background of a non-violent zero level. It is seen as a perturbation of the "normal," peaceful state of things. However, objective violence is precisely the violence inherent to this "normal" state of things. Objective violence is invisible since it sustains the very zero-level standard against which we perceive something as subjectively violent. Systemic violence is thus something like the notorious "dark matter" of physics, the counterpart to an all-too-visible subjective violence. It may be invisible, but it has to be taken into account if one is to make sense of what otherwise seem to be "irrational" explosions of subjective violence.

When the media bombard us with those "humanitarian crises" which seem constantly to pop up all over the world, one should always bear in mind that a particular crisis only explodes into media visibility as the result of a complex struggle. Properly humanitarian considerations as a rule play a less important role here than cultural, ideologico-political, and economic considerations. The cover story of *Time* magazine on 5 June 2006, for example, was "The Deadliest War in the World." This offered detailed documentation on how

around 4 million people died in the Democratic Republic of Congo as the result of political violence over the
last decade. None of the usual humanitarian uproar followed, just a couple of readers' letters–as if some kind of
filtering mechanism blocked this news from achieving
its full impact in our symbolic space. To put it cynically,
Time picked the wrong victim in the struggle for hegemony in suffering. It should have stuck to the list of
usual suspects: Muslim women and their plight, or the
families of 9/11 victims and how they have coped with
their losses. The Congo today has effectively re-emerged
as a Conradean "heart of darkness." No one dares to
confront it head on. The death of a West Bank Palestinian child, not to mention an Israeli or an American, is
mediatically worth thousands of times more than the
death of a nameless Congolese.

Do we need further proof that the humanitarian
sense of urgency is mediated, indeed overdetermined,
by clear political considerations? And what are these
considerations? To answer this, we need to step back
and take a look from a different position. When the U.S.
media reproached the public in foreign countries for
not displaying enough sympathy for the victims of the
9/11 attacks, one was tempted to answer them in the
words Robespierre addressed to those who complained
about the innocent victims of revolutionary terror:
"Stop shaking the tyrant's bloody robe in my face, or I
will believe that you wish to put Rome in chains."[1]

Instead of confronting violence directly, the present book casts six sideways glances. There are reasons
for looking at the problem of violence awry. My underlying premise is that there is something inherently

mystifying in a direct confrontation with it: the over-powering horror of violent acts and empathy with the victims inexorably function as a lure which prevents us from thinking. A *dispassionate* conceptual development of the typology of violence must by definition ignore its traumatic impact. Yet there is a sense in which a cold analysis of violence somehow reproduces and participates in its horror. A distinction needs to be made, as well, between (factual) truth and truthfulness: what renders a report of a raped woman (or any other narrative of a trauma) truthful is its very factual unreliability, its confusion, its inconsistency. If the victim were able to report on her painful and humiliating experience in a clear manner, with all the data arranged in a consistent order, this very quality would make us suspicious of its truth. The problem here is part of the solution: the very factual deficiencies of the traumatised subject's report on her experience bear witness to the truthfulness of her report, since they signal that the reported content "contaminated" the manner of reporting it. The same holds, of course, for the so-called unreliability of the verbal reports of Holocaust survivors: the witness able to offer a clear narrative of his camp experience would disqualify himself by virtue of that clarity.[2] The only appropriate approach to my subject thus seems to be one which permits variations on violence kept at a distance out of respect towards its victims.

Adorno's famous saying, it seems, needs correction: it is not poetry that is impossible after Auschwitz, but rather *prose*.[3] Realistic prose fails, where the poetic evocation of the unbearable atmosphere of a camp succeeds. That is to say, when Adorno declares poetry impossible (or, rather, barbaric) after Auschwitz, this impossibility is an enabling impossibility: poetry is always, by definition, "about" something that cannot be addressed directly, only alluded to. One shouldn't be afraid to take this a step further and refer to the old saying that music comes in when words fail. There may well be some truth in the common wisdom that, in a kind of historical premonition, the music of Schoenberg articulated the anxieties and nightmares of Auschwitz before the event took place.

In her memoirs, Anna Akhmatova describes what happened to her when, at the height of the Stalinist purges, she was waiting in the long queue in front of the Leningrad prison to learn about her arrested son Lev:

> One day somebody in the crowd identified me. Standing behind me was a young woman, with lips blue from the cold, who had of course never heard me called by name before. Now she started out of the torpor common to us all and asked me in a whisper (everyone whispered there), "Can you describe this?" And I said, "I can." Then something like a smile passed fleetingly over what had once been her face.[4]

The key question, of course, is what kind of description is intended here? Surely it is not a realistic description of the situation, but what Wallace Stevens called "description without place," which is what is proper to art. This is not a description which locates its content in a historical space and time, but a description which creates, as the background of the phenomena it describes, an inexistent (virtual) space of its own, so that what appears in it is not an appearance sustained by the depth of reality behind it, but a decontextualised appearance, an appearance which fully coincides with real being. To quote Stevens again: "What it seems it is and in such seeming all things are." Such an artistic description "is not a sign for something that lies outside its form."[5] Rather, it extracts from the confused reality its own inner form in the same way that Schoenberg "extracted" the inner form of totalitarian terror. He evoked the way this terror affects subjectivity.

Does this recourse to artistic description imply that we are in danger of regressing to a contemplative attitude that somehow betrays the urgency to "do something" about the depicted horrors?

Let's think about the fake sense of urgency that pervades the left-liberal humanitarian discourse on violence: in it, abstraction and graphic (pseudo)concreteness coexist in the staging of the scene of violence–against women, blacks, the homeless, gays ... "A woman is raped every six seconds in this country" and "In the time it takes you to read this paragraph, ten children will die of hunger" are just two examples. Underlying all this is a hypocritical sentiment of moral outrage. Just this kind of pseudo-urgency was exploited by Starbucks a couple of years ago when, at store entrances, posters greeting customers pointed out that a portion of the chain's profits went into health-care for the children of Guatemala, the source of their coffee, the inference being that with every cup you drink, you save a child's life.

There is a fundamental anti-theoretical edge to these urgent injunctions. There is no time to reflect: we have to *act now*. Through this fake sense of urgency, the post-industrial rich, living in their secluded virtual world, not only do not deny or ignore the harsh reality outside their area–they actively refer to it all the time. As Bill Gates recently put it: "What do computers matter when millions are still unnecessarily dying of dysentery?"

Against this fake urgency, we might want to place Marx's wonderful letter to Engels of 1870, when, for a brief moment, it seemed that a European revolution was again at the gates. Marx's letter conveys his sheer panic: can't the revolutionaries wait for a couple of years? He hasn't yet finished his *Capital*.

A critical analysis of the present global constellation–one which offers no clear solution, no "practical" advice on what to do, and provides no light at the end of the tunnel, since one is well aware that this light might belong to a train crashing towards us–usually meets with reproach: "Do you mean we should do *nothing*? Just sit and wait?" One should gather the courage to answer: "YES, precisely that!" There are situations when the only truly "practical" thing to do is to resist the temptation to engage immediately and to "wait and see" by means of a patient, critical analysis. Engagement seems to exert its pressure on us from all directions. In a well-known passage from his *Existentialism and Humanism,* Sartre deployed the dilemma of a young man in France in 1942, torn between the duty to help his lone, ill mother and the duty to enter the Resistance and fight the Germans; Sartre's point is, of course, that there is no a priori answer to this dilemma. The young man needs to make a decision grounded only in his own abyssal freedom and assume full responsibility for it.[6]

An obscene third way out of the dilemma would have been to advise the young man to tell his mother that he will join the Resistance, and to tell his Resistance friends that he will take care of his mother, while, in reality, withdrawing to a secluded place and studying . . .

There is more than cheap cynicism in this advice. It brings to mind a well-known Soviet joke about Lenin. Under socialism, Lenin's advice to young people, his answer to what they should do, was "Learn, learn, and learn." This was evoked at all times and displayed on all school walls. The joke goes: Marx, Engels, and Lenin are asked whether they would prefer to have a wife or a mistress. As expected, Marx, rather conservative in private matters, answers, "A wife!" while Engels, more of a *bon vivant,* opts for a mistress. To everyone's surprise, Lenin says, "I'd like to have both!" Why? Is there a hidden stripe of decadent *jouisseur* behind his austere revolutionary image? No–he explains: "So that I can tell my wife that I am going to my mistress, and my mistress that I have to be with my wife . . ." "And then, what do you do?" "I go to a solitary place to learn, learn, and learn!"

Is this not exactly what Lenin did after the catastrophe of 1914? He withdrew to a lonely place in Switzerland, where he "learned, learned, and learned," reading Hegel's logic. And this is what we should do today when we find ourselves bombarded with mediatic images of violence. We need to "learn, learn, and learn" what causes this violence.

1

Adagio ma non troppo e molto espressivo

SOS VIOLENCE

Violence: Subjective and Objective

In 1922 the Soviet government organised the forced ex-pulsion of leading anti-communist intellectuals, from philosophers and theologians to economists and historians. They left Russia for Germany on a boat known as the *Philosophy Steamer.* Prior to his expulsion, Nikolai Lossky, one of those forced into exile, had enjoyed with his family the comfortable life of the haute bourgeoisie, supported by servants and nannies. He

> simply couldn't understand who would want to destroy
> his way of life. What had the Losskys and their kind
> done? His boys and their friends, as they inherited the
> best of what Russia had to offer, helped fill the world
> with talk of literature and music and art, and they led
> gentle lives. What was wrong with that?[1]

While Lossky was without doubt a sincere and be-nevolent person, really caring for the poor and trying to civilise Russian life, such an attitude betrays a breath-taking insensitivity to the *systemic* violence that had to go on in order for such a comfortable life to be possible. We're talking here of the violence inherent in a system: not only direct physical violence, but also the more sub-tle forms of coercion that sustain relations of domina-tion and exploitation, including the threat of violence. The Losskys and their kind effectively "did nothing bad." There was no subjective evil in their life, just the invisible background of this systemic violence. "Then suddenly, into this almost Proustian world . . . Leninism broke in. The day Andrei Lossky was born, in May 1917, the family could hear the sound of riderless horses galloping down neighboring Ivanovskaya Street."[2] Such ominous intrusions multiplied. Once, in his school, Lossky's son was brutally taunted by a working-class schoolmate who shouted at him that "the days of him and his family are over now . . ." In their benevolent-gentle innocence, the Losskys perceived such signs of the forthcoming catastrophe as emerging out of no-where, as signals of an incomprehensibly malevolent new spirit. What they didn't understand was that in the guise of this irrational subjective violence, they were getting back the message they themselves sent out in its inverted true form. It is this violence which seems to arise "out of nowhere" that, perhaps, fits what Walter Benjamin, in his "Critique of Violence," called pure, divine violence.[3]

Opposing all forms of violence, from direct, physical violence (mass murder, terror) to ideological violence (racism, incitement, sexual discrimination), seems to be the main preoccupation of the tolerant liberal attitude that predominates today. An SOS call sustains such talk, drowning out all other approaches: everything else can and has to wait . . . Is there not something suspicious, indeed symptomatic, about this focus on subjective violence–that violence which is enacted by social agents, evil individuals, disciplined repressive apparatuses, fanatical crowds? Doesn't it desperately try to distract our attention from the true locus of trouble, by obliterating from view other forms of violence and thus actively participating in them? According to a well-known anecdote, a German officer visited Picasso in his Paris studio during the Second World War. There he saw *Guernica* and, shocked at the modernist "chaos" of the painting, asked Picasso: "Did you do this?" Picasso calmly replied: "No, *you* did this!" Today, many a liberal, when faced with violent outbursts such as the recent looting in the suburbs of Paris, asks the few remaining leftists who still count on a radical social transformation: "Isn't it *you* who did this? Is *this* what you want?" And we should reply, like Picasso: "No, *you* did this! This is the true result of *your* politics!"

There is an old joke about a husband who returns home earlier than usual from work and finds his wife in bed with another man. The surprised wife exclaims: "Why have you come back early?" The husband furiously snaps back: "What are you doing in bed with another man?" The wife calmly replies: "I asked you a question first–don't try to squeeze out of it by changing the topic!"[4] The same goes for violence: the task is precisely to *change the topic,* to move from the desperate humanitarian SOS call to stop violence to the analysis of that other SOS, the complex interaction of the three modes of violence: subjective, objective, and symbolic. The lesson is thus that one should resist the fascination of subjective violence, of violence enacted by social agents, evil individuals, disciplined repressive apparatuses, fanatical crowds: subjective violence is just the most visible of the three.

～

The notion of objective violence needs to be thoroughly historicised: it took on a new shape with capitalism. Marx described the mad, self-enhancing circulation of capital, whose solipsistic path of parthenogenesis reaches its apogee in today's meta-reflexive speculations on futures. It is far too simplistic to claim that the spectre of this self-engendering monster that pursues its path disregarding any human or environmental concern is an ideological abstraction and that behind this abstraction there are real people and natural objects on whose productive capacities and resources capital's circulation is based and on which it feeds like a gigantic parasite. The problem is that this "abstraction" is not only in our financial speculators' misperception of social reality, but that it is "real" in the precise sense of determining the structure of the material social processes: the fate of whole strata of the population and sometimes of whole countries can be decided by the "solipsistic" speculative dance of capital, which pursues its goal of profitability in blessed indifference to how its movement will affect social reality. So Marx's point is not primarily to reduce this second dimension to the first one, that is, to demonstrate how the theological mad dance of commodities arises out of the antagonisms of "real life." Rather his point is that *one cannot properly grasp the first (the social reality of material production and social interaction) without the second*: it is the self-propelling metaphysical dance of capital that runs the show, that provides the key to real-life developments and catastrophes. Therein resides the fundamental systemic violence of capitalism, much more uncanny than any direct precapitalist socio-ideological violence: this violence is no longer attributable to concrete individuals and their "evil" intentions, but is purely "objective," systemic, anonymous. Here we encounter the Lacanian difference between reality and the Real: "reality" is the social reality of the actual people involved in interaction and in the productive processes, while the Real is the inexorable "abstract," spectral logic of capital that determines what goes on in social reality. One can experience this gap in a palpable way when one visits a country where life is obviously in shambles. We see a lot of ecological decay and human misery. However, the economist's report that one reads afterwards informs us that the country's economic situation is "financially sound" – reality doesn't matter, what matters is the situation of capital . . .

Is this not truer than ever today? Do phenomena usually designated as those of virtual capitalism (the futures trade and similar abstract financial speculations) not point towards the reign of the "real abstraction" at its purest, far more radical than in Marx's time? In short, the highest form of ideology does not reside in getting caught in ideological spectrality, forgetting about its foundation in real people and their relations, but precisely in overlooking this Real of spectrality and in pretending directly to address "real people with their real worries." Visitors to the London Stock Exchange get a free leaflet which explains that the stock market is not about mysterious fluctuations, but about real people and their products. This really is ideology at its purest.

Hegel's fundamental rule is that "objective"

excess–the direct reign of abstract universality which imposes its law mechanically and with utter disregard for the concerned subject caught in its web–is always supplemented by "subjective" excess–the irregular, arbitrary exercise of whims. An exemplary case of this interdependence is provided by Etienne Balibar, who distinguishes two opposite but complementary modes of excessive violence: the "ultra-objective" or systemic violence that is inherent in the social conditions of global capitalism, which involve the "automatic" creation of excluded and dispensable individuals from the homeless to the unemployed, and the "ultra-subjective" violence of newly emerging ethnic and/or religious, in short racist, "fundamentalisms."[5]

Our blindness to the results of systemic violence is perhaps most clearly perceptible in debates about communist crimes. Responsibility for communist crimes is easy to allocate: we are dealing with subjective evil, with agents who did wrong. We can even identify the ideological sources of the crimes–totalitarian ideology, *The Communist Manifesto*, Rousseau, even Plato. But when one draws attention to the millions who died as the result of capitalist globalisation, from the tragedy of Mexico in the sixteenth century through to the Belgian Congo holocaust a century ago, responsibility is largely denied. All this seems just to have happened as the result of an "objective" process, which nobody planned and executed and for which there was no "Capitalist Manifesto." (The one who came closest to writing it was Ayn Rand.)[6] The fact that the Belgian king Leopold II who presided over the Congo holocaust was a great humanitarian and proclaimed a saint by the Pope cannot be dismissed as a mere case of ideological hypocrisy and cynicism. Subjectively, he may well have been a sincere humanitarian, even modestly counteracting the catastrophic consequences of the vast economic project which was the ruthless exploitation of the natural resources of the Congo over which he presided. The country was his personal fiefdom! The ultimate irony is that even most of the profits from this endeavour were for the benefit of the Belgian people, for public works, museums, and so on. King Leopold was surely the precursor of today's "liberal communists," including . . .

The Good Men from Porto Davos

In the last decade, Davos and Porto Alegre figured as the twin cities of globalisation. Davos, an exclusive Swiss resort, is where the global elite of managers, statesmen, and media personalities meet under heavy police protection, in conditions of a state of siege, and try to convince us and themselves that globalisation is its own best remedy. Porto Alegre is the sub-tropical Brazilian town where the counter-elite of the anti-globalisation movement meet, and try to convince us and themselves that capitalist globalisation is not our fate, that—as the official slogan puts it—"another world is possible." Over these last years, however, the Porto Alegre reunions seem somehow to have lost their impetus. We hear less and less of them. Where have the bright stars of Porto Alegre gone?

Some of them, at least, went to Davos. What increasingly gives the predominant tone to Davos meetings is the group of entrepreneurs, some of whom ironically refer to themselves as "liberal communists," who no longer accept the opposition between Davos (global capitalism) and Porto Alegre (the new social movements alternative to global capitalism). Their claim is that we can have the global capitalist cake, i.e., thrive as profitable entrepreneurs, and eat it, too, i.e., endorse the anti-capitalist causes of social responsibility and ecological concern. No need for Porto Alegre, since Davos itself can become Porto Davos.

The new liberal communists are, of course, our usual suspects: Bill Gates and George Soros, the CEOs of Google, IBM, Intel, eBay, as well as their court philosophers, most notably the journalist Thomas Friedman. What makes this group interesting is that their ideology has become all but indistinguishable from the new breed of anti-globalist leftist radicals: Toni Negri himself, the guru of the postmodern left, praises digital capitalism as containing *in nuce* all the elements of communism—one has only to drop the capitalist form, and the revolutionary goal is achieved. Both the old right, with its ridiculous belief in authority and order and parochial patriotism, and the old left with its capitalised Struggle against Capitalism, are today's true conservatives fighting their shadow-theatre struggles and out of touch with the new realities. The signifier of this new reality in the liberal communist Newspeak is "smart": smart indicates the dynamic and nomadic as against centralised bureaucracy; dialogue and cooperation against hierarchical authority; flexibility against routine; culture and knowledge against old industrial production;

spontaneous interaction and autopoiesis against fixed hierarchy.

Bill Gates is the icon of what he has called "frictionless capitalism," a post-industrial society in which we witness the "end of labor," in which software is winning over hardware and the young nerd over the older dark-suited manager. In the new company headquarters, there is little external discipline. Former hackers who dominate the scene work long hours and enjoy free drinks in green surroundings. A crucial feature of Gates as icon is that he is perceived as the ex-hacker who made it. One needs to confer on the term "hacker" all its subversive/marginal/anti-establishment connotations. Hackers want to disturb the smooth functioning of large bureaucratic corporations. At the fantasmatic level, the underlying notion here is that Gates is a subversive, marginal hooligan who has taken over and dressed himself up as a respectable chairman.

Liberal communists are big executives recuperating the spirit of contest, or, to put it the other way round, counter-cultural geeks who take over big corporations. Their dogma is a new, postmodernised version of Adam Smith's old invisible hand of the market. Market and social responsibility here are not opposites. They can be reunited for mutual benefit. As Thomas Friedman, one of their gurus, puts it, nobody has to be vile in order to do business; collaboration with and participation of the employees, dialogue with customers, respect for the environment, transparency of deals, are nowadays the keys to success. In a perceptive account, Olivier Malnuit enumerates the ten commandments of the liberal communist:

1. Give everything away for free (free access, no copyright . . .); just charge for the additional services, which will make you even richer.
2. Change the world, don't just sell things: global revolution, a change of society will make things better.
3. Be caring, sharing, and aware of social responsibility.
4. Be creative: focus on design, new technologies, and sciences.
5. Tell it all: there should be no secrets. Endorse and practise the cult of transparency, the free flow of information, all humanity should collaborate and interact.
6. Don't work and take on a fixed nine-to-five job. Just engage in improvised smart, dynamic, flexible communications.
7. Go back to school and engage in permanent education.
8. Act as an enzyme: work not only for the market, but trigger new forms of social collaborations.
9. Die poor: return your wealth to those who need it, since you have more than you can ever spend.
10. Stand in for the state: practise the partnership of companies with the state.[7]

Liberal communists are pragmatic. They hate a doctrinaire approach. For them there is no single exploited working class today. There are only concrete problems to be solved: starvation in Africa, the plight of Muslim women, religious fundamentalist violence. When there is a humanitarian crisis in Africa–and liberal communists really love humanitarian crises, which bring out the best in them!–there is no point in engaging in old-style anti-imperialist rhetoric. Instead, all of us should just concentrate on what really does the work of solving the problem: engage people, governments, and business in a common enterprise; start moving things, instead of relying on centralised state help; approach the crisis in a creative and unconventional way, without fretting over labels.

Liberal communists like examples such as the struggle against apartheid in South Africa. They point out that the decision of some large international corporations to ignore apartheid rules in their South African companies, abolishing all segregation, paying blacks and whites the same salary for the same job, and so on, was as important as the direct political struggle. Is this not an ideal case of the overlapping between the struggle for political freedom and business interests? The self-same companies can now thrive in post-apartheid South Africa.

Liberal communists also love the student protests which shattered France in May 1968: what an explosion of youthful energy and creativity! How it shattered the confines of the rigid bureaucratic order! What new impetus it gave to economic and social life, once the political illusions dropped away! After all, many of them were young then, protesting and fighting cops on the streets. If they've changed now, it's not because they resigned themselves to reality, but because they needed to change in order *really* to change the world, *really* to revolutionise our lives. Hadn't Marx already asked: what are political upheavals in comparison with the invention of the steam engine? Didn't this do more than all revolutions to change our lives? And would Marx not have said today: what are all the protests against global capitalism worth in comparison with the invention of the internet?

Above all, liberal communists are true citizens of the world. They are good people who worry. They worry about populist fundamentalists *and* irresponsible, greedy capitalist corporations. They see the "deeper causes" of today's problems: it is mass poverty and hopelessness which breed fundamentalist terror. So their goal is not to earn money, but to change the world, though if this makes them more money as a by-product, who's to complain! Bill Gates is already the single greatest benefactor in the history of humanity, displaying his love for neighbours with hundreds of millions freely given to education, and the battles against hunger and malaria. The catch, of course, is that in order to give, first you have to take–or, as some would put it, create. The justification of liberal communists is that in order to really help people, you must have the means to do it, and as experience of the dismal failure of all centralised statist and collectivist approaches teaches, private initiative is the efficient way. So if the state wants to regulate their business, to tax them excessively, is it aware that in this way it is effectively undermining the stated goal of its activity–that is, to make life better for the large majority, to really help those in need?

Liberal communists do not want to be just machines for generating profits. They want their lives to have a deeper meaning. They are against old-fashioned religion, but for spirituality, for non-confessional meditation. Everybody knows that Buddhism foreshadows the brain sciences, that the power of meditation can be measured scientifically! Their preferred motto is social responsibility and gratitude: they are the first to admit that society was incredibly good to them by allowing them to deploy their talents and amass wealth, so it is their duty to give something back to society and help people. After all, what is the point of their success, if not to help people? It is only this caring that makes business success worthwhile . . .

We need to ask ourselves whether there really is something new here. Is it not merely that an attitude which, in the wild old capitalist days of the U.S. industrial barons, was something of an exception (although not as much as it may appear) has now gained universal currency? Good old Andrew Carnegie employed a private army brutally to suppress organised labour in his steelworks and then distributed large parts of his wealth to educational, artistic, and humanitarian causes. A man of steel, he proved he had a heart of gold. In the same way, today's liberal communists give away with one hand what they first took with the other. This brings to mind a chocolate laxative available in the U.S. It is publicised with the paradoxical injunction: "Do you have constipation? Eat more of this chocolate!" In other words, eat the very thing that causes constipation in order to be cured of it.

The same structure–the thing itself is the remedy against the threat it poses–is widely visible in today's ideological landscape. Take the figure of the financier and philanthropist George Soros, for instance. Soros stands for the most ruthless financial speculative exploitation combined with its counter-agent, humanitarian concern about the catastrophic social consequences of an unbridled market economy. Even his daily routine is marked by a self-eliminating counterpoint: half of his working time is devoted to financial speculation and the other half to humanitarian activities – such as providing finance for cultural and democratic activities in post-communist countries, writing essays and books – which ultimately fight the effects of his own speculation.

The two faces of Bill Gates parallel the two faces of Soros. The cruel businessman destroys or buys out competitors, aims at virtual monopoly, employs all the tricks of the trade to achieve his goals. Meanwhile, the greatest philanthropist in the history of mankind quaintly asks: "What does it serve to have computers, if people do not have enough to eat and are dying of dysentery?" In liberal communist ethics, the ruthless pursuit of profit is counteracted by charity. Charity is the humanitarian mask hiding the face of economic exploitation. In a superego blackmail of gigantic proportions, the developed countries "help" the undeveloped with aid, credits, and so on, and thereby avoid the key issue, namely their complicity in and co-responsibility for the miserable situation of the undeveloped.[8]

Referring to Georges Bataille's notion of the "general economy" of sovereign expenditure, which he opposes to the "restrained economy" of capitalism's endless profiteering, the German post-humanist philosopher Peter Sloterdijk provides the outlines of capitalism's split from itself, its immanent self-overcoming: capitalism culminates when it "creates out of itself its own most radical–and the only fruitful–opposite, totally different from what the classic Left, caught in its miserabilism, was able to dream about."[9] His positive mention of Andrew Carnegie shows the way; the sovereign self-negating gesture of the endless accumulation of wealth is to spend this wealth for things beyond price, and outside market circulation: public good, arts and sciences, health, etc. This concluding "sovereign" gesture enables the capitalist to break out of the vicious cycle of endless expanded reproduction, of gaining money in order to earn more money. When he donates his accumulated wealth to public good, the capitalist self-negates himself as the mere personification of capital and its reproductive circulation: his life acquires meaning. It is no longer just expanded reproduction as self-goal. Furthermore, the capitalist thus accomplishes the shift from *eros* to *thymos,* from the perverted "erotic" logic of accumulation to public recognition and reputation. What this amounts to is nothing less than elevating figures like Soros or Gates to personifications of the inherent self-negation of the capitalist process itself: their work of charity–their immense donations to public welfare–is not just a personal idiosyncrasy. Whether sincere or hypocritical, it is the logical concluding point of capitalist circulation, necessary from the strictly economic standpoint, since it allows the capitalist system to postpone its crisis. It re-establishes balance–a kind of redistribution of wealth to the truly needy–without falling into a fateful trap: the destructive logic of resentment and enforced statist redistribution of wealth which can only end in generalised misery. It also avoids, one might add, the other mode of re-establishing a kind of balance and asserting *thymos* through sovereign expenditure, namely wars . . .

This paradox signals a sad predicament of ours: today's capitalism cannot reproduce itself on its own. It needs extra-economic charity to sustain the cycle of social reproduction.

A Liberal-Communist Village

It is the merit of M. Night Shyamalan's *The Village* that it renders the liberal-communist way of life, based on fear, at its purest. Those who all too easily dismiss Shyamalan's films as the lowest of New Age kitsch are in for some surprises here. The eponymous village in Pennsylvania is cut off from the rest of the world and surrounded by woods full of dangerous monsters, known to the villagers as "Those We Don't Speak Of." Most villagers are content to live by the bargain they made with the creatures: they don't enter the forest, the creatures don't enter the town. Conflict arises when the young Lucius Hunt wishes to leave the village in search of new medicines and the pact is broken. Lucius and Ivy Walker, the village leader's blind daughter, decide to get married. This makes the village idiot madly jealous; he stabs Lucius and nearly kills him, leaving him at the mercy of an infection that requires medicine from the outside world. Ivy's father then tells her about the town's secret: there are no monsters, and the year isn't really 1897. The town elders were part of a twentieth-century crime victims' support group which decided to withdraw from the century completely; Walker's father had been a millionaire businessman, so they bought land, called it a "wildlife preserve," surrounded it with

a big fence and lots of guards, bribed government offi-
cials to reroute aeroplanes away from the community,
and moved inside, concocting the story about "Those
We Don't Speak Of" to keep anyone from leaving. With
her father's blessing, Ivy slips outside, meets a friendly
security guard who gives her some medicine, and returns to save her betrothed's life. At the film's end, the
village elders decide to go on with their secluded lives:
the village idiot's death can be presented to the uninitiated as proof that monsters exist, thereby confirming
the founding myth of the community. Sacrificial logic
is reasserted as the condition of community, as its secret bond.

No wonder most critics dismissed the film as the
worst case of ideological cocooning: "It's easy to understand why he's attracted to setting a movie in a period where people proclaimed their emotions in full
and heartfelt sentences, or why he enjoys building a
village that's impenetrable to the outside world. He's
not making movies. He's making cocoons."[10] Underlying the film is thus the desire to recreate a closed universe of authenticity in which innocence is protected
from the corrosive force of modernity: "It's all about
how to protect your innocence from getting hurt by
the 'creatures' in your life; the desire to protect your
children from going into the unknown. If these 'creatures' have hurt you, you don't want them to hurt your
children and the younger generation may be willing to
risk that."[11]

A closer look reveals the film to be much more ambiguous. When reviewers noticed that "the movie is in
H. P. Lovecraft territory: severe, wintry New England

palette; a suggestion of inbreeding; hushed mentions of 'the Old Ones,' 'Those We Don't Speak Of,' "[12] as a rule they forgot to note the political context. The late-nineteenth-century self-subsistent community evokes the many utopian-socialist experiments that sprang up in America. This does not mean that the Lovecraft reference to supernatural horror is just a mask or a false lure. We have two universes: the modern, open "risk society" versus the safety of the old secluded universe of Meaning–but the price of Meaning is a finite, closed space guarded by unnameable monsters. Evil is not simply excluded in this closed utopian space–it is transformed into a mythic threat with which the community establishes a temporary truce and against which it has to maintain a permanent state of emergency.

The "Deleted Scenes" special feature on a DVD release all too often makes the viewer realise that the director was only too right to delete them. The DVD edition of *The Village* is an exception. One of the deleted scenes shows a drill: Walker rings the bell, which signals a speedy practice retreat into underground shelters. Here is where the people must go in the event that the creatures attack. It is as if authentic community is possible only in conditions of permanent threat, in a continuous state of emergency.[13] This threat is orchestrated, as we learn, in the best "totalitarian" manner by the inner circle, the "elders" of the community itself, in order to prevent the uninitiated youngsters from leaving the village and risking the passage through the forest to the decadent towns. Evil itself has to be redoubled: the "real" evil of late-capitalist social disintegration has to be transposed into the archaic magic-mythic evil of "monsters." The evil is a part of the inner circle itself: it is *imagined* by its members. We seem to be back, here, with G. K. Chesterton's *The Man Who Was Thursday,* in which the highest police authority *is* the same person as the super-criminal, staging a battle with himself. In a proto-Hegelian way, the external threat the community is fighting is its own inherent essence . . .[14]

And what if this is true in a much more radical way than may at first appear? What if the true evil of our societies is not their capitalist dynamics as such, but our attempts to extricate ourselves from them–all the while profiting–by carving out self-enclosed communal spaces, from "gated communities" to exclusive racial or religious groups? That is to say, is the point of *The Village* not precisely to demonstrate that today, a return to an authentic community in which speech still directly expresses true emotions–the village of the socialist utopia–is a fake which can only be staged as a spectacle for the very rich? The exemplary figures of evil today are not ordinary consumers who pollute the environment and live in a violent world of disintegrating social links, but those who, while fully engaged in creating conditions for such universal devastation and pollution, buy their way out of their own activity, living in gated communities, eating organic food, taking holidays in wildlife preserves, and so on.

In Alfonso Cuarón's film *Children of Men,* based on the P. D. James novel, the liberal-communist village is the United Kingdom itself. It is 2027. The human race is infertile. The earth's youngest inhabitant, born eighteen years earlier, has just been killed in Buenos Aires. The U.K. lives in a permanent state of emergency: anti-terrorist squads chase illegal immigrants, the state power administering a dwindling population which vegetates in sterile hedonism. Hedonist permissiveness plus new forms of social apartheid and control based on fear—are these not what our societies are now about? But here is Cuarón's stroke of genius: "Many of the stories of the future involve something like 'Big Brother,' but I think that's a twentieth-century view of tyranny. The tyranny happening now is taking new disguises—the tyranny of the twenty-first century is called 'democracy.'"[15] This is why the rulers of Cuarón's world are not grey and uniformed Orwellian "totalitarian" bureaucrats, but enlightened, democratic administrators, cultured, each with his or her own "life style." When the hero visits an ex-friend, now a top government official, to gain a special permit for a refugee, we enter something like a Manhattan upper-class gay couple's loft, the informally dressed official with his crippled partner at the table.

Children of Men is obviously not a film about infertility as a biological problem. The infertility Cuarón's film is about was diagnosed long ago by Friedrich Nietzsche, when he perceived how Western civilisation was moving in the direction of the Last Man, an apathetic creature with no great passion or commitment. Unable to dream, tired of life, he takes no risks, seeking only comfort and security, an expression of tolerance with one another: "A little poison now and then: that makes for pleasant dreams. And much poison at the end, for a pleasant death. They have their little pleasures for the day, and their little pleasures for the night, but they have a regard for health. 'We have discovered happiness,'–say the Last Men, and they blink."[16]

We from the First World countries find it more and more difficult even to imagine a public or universal cause for which one would be ready to sacrifice one's life. Indeed, the split between First and Third World runs increasingly along the lines of an opposition between leading a long, satisfying life full of material and cultural wealth, and dedicating one's life to some transcendent cause. Isn't this the antagonism between what Nietzsche called "passive" and "active" nihilism? We in the West are the Last Men, immersed in stupid daily pleasures, while the Muslim radicals are ready to risk everything, engaged in the nihilist struggle up to the point of self-destruction. What is gradually disappearing in this opposition between those who are "in," the Last Men who dwell in aseptic gated communities, and those who are "out," are the good old middle classes. The "middle class is a luxury capitalism can no longer afford."[17] The only place in *Children of Men* where a strange sense of freedom prevails is Bexhill on Sea, a kind of liberated territory outside the all-pervasive and suffocating oppression. The town, isolated by a wall and turned into a refugee camp, is run by its inhabitants, who are illegal immigrants. Life is thriving here with Islamic fundamentalist military demonstrations, but also with acts of authentic solidarity. No wonder that rare creature, the newborn child, makes its appearance here. At the film's end, this Bexhill on Sea is ruthlessly bombed by the air force.

Sexuality in the Atonal World

What kind of sexuality fits this universe? On 6 August 2006 London hosted the U.K.'s first "masturbate-a-thon," a collective event in which hundreds of men and women pleasured themselves for charity, raising money for sexual and reproductive health agencies. They also raised awareness and dispelled the shame and taboos that persist around this most commonplace, natural, and safe form of sexual activity. The formula was invented at Good Vibrations–a San Francisco sexual-health company–as part of a National Masturbation Month, which they founded and have been hosting since 1995 when the original San Francisco M-A-T took place. Here is how Dr. Carol Queen justifies it all:

> We live in a society in which sexual expression has always been legislated and restricted and the pursuit of pure pleasure is frequently condemned as selfish and childish. A lot of people who consider themselves free of sexual hang-ups have simply rewritten the equation "sex is only good if it involves procreation" to "sex is only good if it involves two loving people" . . . Masturbation is our first sexual activity, a natural source of pleasure that's available to us throughout our lives, and a unique form of creative self-expression. Each time you masturbate, you're celebrating your sexuality and your innate capacity for pleasure, so give yourself a hand! . . . Masturbation can be a radical act, and the culture that suppresses masturbation may suppress many other personal freedoms as well. While celebrating National Masturbation Month and doing

your part to bring self-love out of the closet, keep in mind that erotic freedom is essential to true well-being, everywhere.[18]

The ideological stance underlying the notion of the masturbate-a-thon is marked by a conflict between its form and content: it builds a collective out of individuals who are ready to *share* with others the solipsistic egotism of their stupid pleasure. This contradiction, however, is more apparent than real. Freud already knew about the link between narcissism and immersion in a crowd, best rendered precisely by the Californian phrase "to share an experience." This coincidence of opposed features is grounded in the exclusion that they share: one not only can be, one *is* alone in a crowd. Both an individual's isolation and his immersion in a crowd exclude intersubjectivity proper, the encounter with an Other. This is why, as the French philosopher Alain Badiou set out in a perspicuous way, today more than ever one should insist on a focus on love, not mere enjoyment: it is love, the encounter of the Two, which "transubstantiates" idiotic masturbatory enjoyment into an event proper.[19] A minimally refined sensitivity tells us that it is more difficult to masturbate in front of an other than to be engaged in a sexual interaction with him or her: the very fact that the other is reduced to an observer, not participating in my activity, makes my act much more "shameful." Events such as the masturbate-a-thon signal the end of shame proper. This is what makes it one of the clearest indications of where we stand today, of an ideology which sustains our most intimate self-experience.

"Why masturbate?" Here is the list of reasons proposed by Queen:

➤ Because sexual pleasure is each person's birthright.
➤ Because masturbation is the ultimate safe sex.
➤ Because masturbation is a joyous expression of self-love.
➤ Because masturbation offers numerous health benefits including menstrual cramp relief, stress reduction, endorphin release, stronger pelvic muscles, reduction of prostate gland infection for men, and resistance to yeast infections for women.
➤ Because masturbation is an excellent cardiovascular workout.
➤ Because each person is their own best lover.
➤ Because masturbation increases sexual awareness.

Everything is here: increased self-awareness, health benefits, struggle against social oppression, the most radical politically correct stance (here, it's certain that nobody is harassed), and the affirmation of sexual pleasure at its most elementary–"each person is their own best lover." The use of the expression usually reserved for homosexuals (masturbation "brings self-love out of the closet") hints at a kind of implicit teleology of the gradual exclusion of all otherness: first, in homosexuality, the other sex is excluded (one does it with another person of the same sex). Then, in a kind of mockingly Hegelian negation of negation, the very dimension of otherness is cancelled: one does it with oneself.

In December 2006, the New York City authorities declared that to chose one's gender–and so, if necessary, to have a sex-change operation performed–is one of the inalienable human rights. The ultimate difference, the "transcendental" difference that grounds human identity itself, thus turns into something open to manipulation: the ultimate plasticity of being human is asserted instead. The masturbate-a-thon is the ideal form of sex activity of this transgendered subject, or, in other words, of *you*, the subject *Time* magazine elevated into "Person of the Year" in its 18 December 2006 issue. This annual honour went not to Ahmadinejad, Chavez, Kim Jong-Il, or any other member of the gang of usual suspects, but to "you": each and every one of us who is using or creating content on the World Wide Web. The cover showed a white keyboard with a mirror for a computer screen where each of us readers can see his or her own reflection. To justify the choice, the editors cited the shift from institutions to individuals who are re-emerging as the citizens of the new digital democracy.

There is more than meets the eye in this choice, and in more than the usual sense of the term. If there ever was an *ideological* choice, this is it: the message–a new cyber-democracy in which millions can directly communicate and self-organise, by-passing centralised state control–covers up a series of disturbing gaps and tensions. The first and obvious point of irony is that what everyone who looks at the *Time* cover sees is not others with whom he or she is supposed to be in direct exchange, but their own mirror-image. No wonder that

Leibniz is one of the predominant philosophical references of the cyberspace theorists: does our immersion in cyberspace not go hand in hand with our reduction to a Leibnizean monad which mirrors the entire universe, though "without windows" that would directly open up to external reality? It could be said that the typical World Wide Web surfer today, sitting alone in front of a PC screen, is increasingly a monad with no direct windows onto reality, encountering only virtual simulacra, and yet immersed more than ever in a global communication network. The masturbate-a-thon, which builds a collective out of individuals who are ready to share the solipsism of their own stupid enjoyment, is the form of sexuality which fits these cyberspace coordinates perfectly.

Alain Badiou develops the notion of "atonal" worlds—*monde atone*—which lack the intervention of a Master-Signifier to impose meaningful order onto the confused multiplicity of reality.[20] What is a Master-Signifier?[21] In the very last pages of his monumental *Second World War*, Winston Churchill ponders on the enigma of a political decision: after the specialists—economic and military analysts, psychologists, meteorologists—propose their multiple, elaborated, and refined analyses, somebody must assume the simple and for that very reason most difficult act of transposing this complex multitude of views, where for every reason for, there are two reasons against and vice versa, into a simple, decisive Yes or No. We shall attack or we continue to wait. None other than John F. Kennedy provided a concise description of this point: "the essence of ultimate decision remains impenetrable to the observer—often, indeed, to the decider himself." This decisive gesture which can never be fully grounded in reasons is that of a Master.

A basic feature of our postmodern world is that it tries to dispense with this agency of the ordering Master-Signifier: the complexity of the world needs to be asserted unconditionally. Every Master-Signifier meant to impose some order on it must be deconstructed, dispersed: "the modern apology for the 'complexity' of the world . . . is really nothing but a generalized desire for atony."[22] Badiou's excellent example of such an "atonal" world is the politically correct vision of sexuality as promoted by gender studies with its obsessive rejection of binary logic: this world is a nuanced world of multiple sexual practices which tolerates no decision, no instance of the Two, no evaluation, in the strong Nietzschean sense of the term.

Michel Houellebecq's novels are interesting in this context.[23] He endlessly varies the motif of the failure of the event of love in contemporary Western societies characterised, as one reviewer put it, by "the collapse of religion and tradition, the unrestrained worship of pleasure and youth, and the prospect of a future totalized by scientific rationality and joylessness."[24] Here is the dark side of 1960s "sexual liberation": the full commodification of sexuality. Houellebecq depicts the morning-after of the Sexual Revolution, the sterility of a universe dominated by the superego injunction to enjoy. All of his work focuses on the antinomy of love and sexuality: sex is an absolute necessity, to renounce it is to wither away, so love cannot flourish without sex; simultaneously, however, love is impossible precisely because of sex: sex, which "proliferates as the epitome of late capitalism's dominance, has permanently stained human relationships as inevitable reproductions of the dehumanizing nature of liberal society; it has, essentially, ruined love."[25] Sex is thus, to put it in Derridean terms, simultaneously the condition of the possibility and of the impossibility of love.

~

We live in a society where a kind of Hegelian speculative identity of opposites exists. Certain features, attitudes, and norms of life are no longer perceived as ideologically marked. They appear to be neutral, non-ideological, natural, commonsensical. We designate as ideology that which stands out from this background: extreme religious zeal or dedication to a particular political orientation. The Hegelian point here would be that it is precisely the neutralisation of some features into a spontaneously accepted background that marks out ideology at its purest and at its most effective. This is the dialectical "coincidence of opposites": the actualisation of a notion or an ideology at its purest coincides with, or, more precisely, appears as its opposite, as non-ideology. *Mutatis mutandis,* the same holds for violence. Social-symbolic violence at its purest appears as its opposite, as the spontaneity of the milieu in which we dwell, of the air we breathe.

This is why the delicate liberal communist–frightened, caring, fighting violence–and the blind fundamentalist exploding in rage are two sides of the same coin. While they fight subjective violence, liberal communists are the very agents of the structural violence which creates the conditions for the explosions of subjective violence. The same philanthropists who give millions for AIDS or education in tolerance have ruined the lives of thousands through financial speculation and thus created the conditions for the rise of the very intolerance that is being fought. In the 1960s and '70s it was possible to buy soft-porn postcards of a girl clad in a bikini or wearing an evening gown; however, when one moved the postcard a little bit or looked at it from a slightly different perspective, her clothes magically disappeared to reveal the girl's naked body. When we are bombarded by the heartwarming news of a debt cancellation or a big humanitarian campaign to eradicate a dangerous epidemic, just move the postcard a little to catch a glimpse of the obscene figure of the liberal communist at work beneath.

We should have no illusions: liberal communists are the enemy of every progressive struggle today. All other enemies–religious fundamentalists and terrorists, corrupted and inefficient state bureaucracies–are particular figures whose rise and fall depends on contingent local circumstances. Precisely because they want to resolve all the secondary malfunctions of the global system, liberal communists are the direct embodiment of what is wrong with the system as such. This needs to be borne in mind in the midst of the various tactical alliances and compromises one has to make with liberal communists when fighting racism, sexism, and religious obscurantism.

What, then, should be done with our liberal communist who is undoubtedly a good man and really worried about the poverty and violence in the world and can afford his worries? Indeed, what to do with a man who cannot be bought by the corporate interests because he co-owns the corporation; who holds to what he says about fighting poverty because he profits by it; who honestly expresses his opinion because he is so powerful that he can afford to; who is brave and wise in ruthlessly pursuing his enterprises, and does not consider his personal advantages, since all his needs are already satisfied; and who, furthermore, is a good friend, particularly of his Davos colleagues? Bertolt Brecht provided an answer in his poem "The Interrogation of the Good":

> Step forward: we hear
> That you are a good man.
> You cannot be bought, but the lightning
> Which strikes the house, also
> Cannot be bought.
> You hold to what you said.
> But what did you say?
> You are honest, you say your opinion.
> Which opinion?
> You are brave.
> Against whom?
> You are wise.
> For whom?
> You do not consider your personal advantages.
> Whose advantages do you consider then?
> You are a good friend.
> Are you also a good friend of the good people?
>
> Hear us then: we know
> You are our enemy. This is why we shall

Now put you in front of a wall. But in consideration of
    your merits and good qualities
We shall put you in front of a good wall and shoot you
With a good bullet from a good gun and bury you
With a good shovel in the good earth.[26]

2

Allegro moderato–Adagio

FEAR THY NEIGHBOUR AS THYSELF!

The Politics of Fear

Today's predominant mode of politics is *post-political bio-politics*–an awesome example of theoretical jargon which, however, can easily be unpacked: "post-political" is a politics which claims to leave behind old ideological struggles and instead focus on expert management and administration, while "bio-politics" designates the regulation of the security and welfare of human lives as its primary goal.[1] It is clear how these two dimensions overlap: once one renounces big ideological causes, what remains is only the efficient administration of life . . . *almost* only that. That is to say, with the depoliticised, socially objective, expert administration and coordination of interests as the zero level of politics, the only way to introduce passion into this field, to actively mobilise people, is through fear, a basic constituent of today's subjectivity. For this reason, bio-politics is ultimately a politics of fear; it focuses on defence from potential victimisation or harassment.

This is what separates a radical emancipatory politics from our political status quo. We're talking here not about the difference between two visions, or sets of axioms, but about the difference between politics based on a set of universal axioms and a politics which renounces the very constitutive dimension of the political, since it resorts to fear as its ultimate mobilising principle: fear of immigrants, fear of crime, fear of godless sexual depravity, fear of the excessive state itself, with its burden of high taxation, fear of ecological catastrophe, fear of harassment. Political correctness is the exemplary liberal form of the politics of fear. Such a (post-)politics always relies on the manipulation of a paranoid *ochlos* or multitude: it is the frightening rallying of frightened people.

Thus the big event of 2006 was when anti-immigration politics went mainstream and finally cut the umbilical cord that had connected it to far-right fringe parties. From France to Germany, from Austria to Holland, in the new spirit of pride in cultural and historical identity, the main parties now found it acceptable to stress that immigrants are guests who must accommodate themselves to the cultural values that define the host society–"It is our country, love it or leave it."

Today's liberal tolerance towards others, the respect of otherness and openness towards it, is counterpointed by an obsessive fear of harassment. In short, the Other is just fine, but only insofar as his presence is not intrusive, insofar as this Other is not really other . . . In a strict homology with the paradoxical structure of the previous chapter's chocolate laxative, tolerance coincides with its opposite. My duty to be tolerant towards the Other effectively means that I should not get too close to him, intrude on his space. In other words, I should respect his *intolerance* of my over-proximity. What increasingly emerges as the central human right in late-capitalist society is *the right not to be harassed,* which is a right to remain at a safe distance from others.

Post-political bio-politics also has two aspects which cannot but appear to belong to two opposite ideological spaces: that of the reduction of humans to "bare life," to *Homo sacer,* that so-called sacred being who is the object of expert caretaking knowledge, but is excluded, like prisoners at Guantanamo or Holocaust victims, from all rights; and that of respect for the vulnerable Other brought to an extreme through an attitude of narcissistic subjectivity which experiences the self as vulnerable, constantly exposed to a multitude of potential "harassments." Can there be a more emphatic contrast than the one between respect for the Other's vulnerability and the reduction of the Other to mere "bare life" regulated by administrative knowledge? But what if these two stances none the less spring from a single root? What if they are two aspects of one and the same underlying attitude? What if they coincide in what one is tempted to designate as the contemporary case of the Hegelian "infinite judgment" which asserts the identity of opposites? What these two poles share is precisely the underlying refusal of any higher causes, the notion that the ultimate goal of our lives is life itself. This is why there is no contradiction between the respect for the vulnerable Other and the readiness to justify torture, the extreme expression of treating individuals as *Homini sacer.*[2]

In *The End of Faith,* Sam Harris defends the use of torture in exceptional cases (but of course everyone who defends torture defends it as an exceptional measure—nobody seriously advocates torturing a small hungry child who has stolen a chocolate bar). His defence is based on the distinction between our instinctive abhorrence of witnessing the torture or suffering of an individual with our own eyes, and our abstract knowledge of mass suffering: it is much more difficult for us to torture an individual than to sanction from afar the dropping of a bomb which would cause the more painful deaths of thousands.

We are thus all caught in a kind of ethical illusion, parallel to perceptual illusions. The ultimate cause of these illusions is that although our power of abstract reasoning has developed immensely, our emotional-ethical responses remain conditioned by age-old instinctual reactions of sympathy to suffering and pain that is witnessed directly. This is why shooting someone point-blank is for most of us much more repulsive than pressing a button that will kill a thousand people we cannot see:

> Given what many of us believe about the exigencies of our war on terrorism, the practice of torture, in certain circumstances, would seem to be not only permissible but necessary. Still, it does not seem any more acceptable, in ethical terms, than it did before. The reasons for this are, I trust, every bit as neurological as those that give rise to the moon illusion. [. . .] It may be time to take out our rulers and hold them up to the sky.[3]

No wonder that Harris refers to Alan Dershowitz and his legitimisation of torture.[4] In order to suspend this evolutionary conditioned vulnerability to the physical display of others' suffering, Harris imagines an ideal "truth pill," an effective torture equivalent to decaffeinated coffee or diet Coke:

a drug that would deliver both the instruments of torture and the instrument of their utter concealment. The action of the pill would be to produce transitory paralysis and transitory misery of a kind that no human being would willingly submit to a second time. Imagine how we torturers would feel if, after giving this pill to captive terrorists, each lay down for what appeared to be an hour's nap only to arise and immediately confess everything he knows about the workings of his organization. Might we not be tempted to call it a "truth pill" in the end?[5]

The very first words–"a drug that would deliver both the instruments of torture and the instrument of their utter concealment"–introduce the typically postmodern logic of chocolate laxative: the torture imagined here is like decaf coffee–we get the desired result without having to suffer unpleasant side effects. At the notorious Serbsky Institute in Moscow, the psychiatric outlet of the KGB, they did invent just such a drug with which to torture dissidents: an injection into the prisoner's heart zone which slowed his pulse and caused terrifying anxiety. Viewed from the outside, the prisoner seemed just to be dozing, while in fact he was living a nightmare.

Harris violates his own rules when he focuses on September 11, and in his critique of Chomsky. Chomsky's point is precisely that there is a hypocrisy in tolerating the abstract-anonymous killing of thousands, while condemning individual cases of the violation of human rights. Why should Kissinger, when he ordered the carpet bombing of Cambodia that led to the deaths of tens of thousands, be less of a criminal than those responsible for the Twin Towers collapse? Is it not because we are victims of an "ethical illusion"? The horror of September 11 was presented in detail in the media, but al-Jazeera TV was condemned for showing shots of the results of U.S. bombing in Fallujah and condemned for complicity with the terrorists.

There is, however, a much more disquieting prospect at work here: the proximity (of the tortured subject) which causes sympathy and makes torture unacceptable is not the victim's mere physical proximity but, at its most fundamental, the proximity of the Neighbour, with all the Judeo-Christian-Freudian weight of this term, the proximity of the thing which, no matter how far away it is physically, is always by definition "too close." What Harris is aiming at with his imagined "truth pill" is nothing less than *the abolition of the dimension of the Neighbour.* The tortured subject is no longer a Neighbour, but an object whose pain is neutralised, reduced to a property that has to be dealt with in a rational utilitarian calculus (so much pain is tolerable if it prevents a much greater amount of pain). What disappears here is the abyss of the infinity that pertains to a subject. It is thus significant that the book which argues for torture is also a book entitled *The End of Faith*–not in the obvious sense of, "You see, it is only our belief in God, the divine injunction to love your neighbour, that ultimately prevents us from torturing people!," but in a much more radical sense. Another subject (and ultimately the subject as such) is for Lacan not something directly given, but a "presupposition," *something presumed, an object of belief*–how can I ever be sure that what I see in front of me is another subject, not a flat biological machine lacking depth?

The Neighbour Thing

This presupposed subject is thus not another human being with a rich inner life filled with personal stories which are self-narrated in order to acquire a meaningful experience of life, since such a person cannot ultimately be an enemy. "An enemy is someone whose story you have not heard."[6] What better literary example of this thesis than Mary Shelley's *Frankenstein*. Shelley does something that a conservative would never have done. In the central part of her book, she allows the monster to speak for himself, to tell the story from his own perspective. Her choice expresses the liberal attitude to freedom of speech at its most radical: everyone's point of view should be heard. In *Frankenstein*, the monster is not a "thing," a horrible object no one dares to confront; he is fully *subjectivised*. Mary Shelley moves inside his mind and asks what it is like to be labelled, defined, oppressed, excommunicated, even physically distorted by society. The ultimate criminal is thus allowed to present himself as the ultimate victim. The monstrous murderer reveals himself to be a deeply hurt and desperate individual, yearning for company and love.

There is, however, a clear limit to this procedure: is one also ready to affirm that Hitler was an enemy because his story was not heard? In *Lenin's Tomb*, David Remnick reports his attempts, during his visit to Moscow in 1988, to meet Lazar Kaganovich, the last surviving member of Stalin's inner circle, who directed the collectivisation programme of 1929–33 and was responsible for untold destruction and suffering. At the age of ninety-plus, he was living a secluded life in a lonely apartment. What fascinated Remnick was the prospect of seeing a truly evil person:

> Did Kaganovich still believe? I wanted to know. Did he feel any guilt, any shame? And what did he think of Gorbachev, the current general secretary? But that wasn't it, really. Mostly I wanted just to sit in the same room with Kaganovich, to see what an evil man looked like, to know what he did, what books he kept around.[7]

What, in all probability, Remnick would have encountered had he succeeded would have been a frail, benevolent old man stuck in his dreams. When, in the 1960s, Svetlana Stalin emigrated to the U.S. through India and wrote her memoirs, she presented Stalin "from inside" as a warm father and caring leader, with most of the mass murders imposed on him by his evil collaborators, Lavrenty Beria in particular. Later, Beria's son Sergo wrote a memoir presenting his father as a warm family man who simply followed Stalin's orders and secretly tried to limit the damage. Georgy Malenkov's son Andrei also told his story, describing his father, Stalin's successor, as an honest hard worker, always afraid for his life. Hannah Arendt was right: these figures were not personifications of sublime Byronesque demonic evil: the gap between their intimate experience and the horror of their acts was immense. The experience that we have of our lives from within, the story we tell ourselves about ourselves in order to account for what we are doing, is fundamentally a lie–the truth lies outside, in what we do.[8]

One thing that never ceases to surprise the naive ethical consciousness is how the very same people who commit terrible acts of violence towards their enemies can display warm humanity and gentle care for the members of their own group. Isn't it strange that the same soldier who slaughtered innocent civilians was ready to sacrifice his life for his unit? That the commander who ordered the shooting of hostages can that same evening write a letter to his family full of sincere love? This limitation of our ethical concern to a narrow circle seems to run counter to our spontaneous insight that we are all humans, with the same basic hopes, fears, and pains, and therefore the same justified claim to respect and dignity. Consequently, those who constrain the scope of their ethical concern are in a profound sense inconsistent, "hypocritical" even. To put it in Habermasian terms, they are involved in a pragmatic contradiction, since they violate the ethical norms which sustain their own speech community. Refusing the same basic ethical rights to those outside our community as to those inside it is something that does not come naturally to a human being. It is a violation of our spontaneous ethical proclivity. It involves brutal repression and self-denial.

When, after the fall of communism, the East German soft-dissident writer Stephan Hermlin was reproached for writing texts and poems back in the 1950s that celebrated Stalin, he replied with furious indignity that in those years in Europe the name "Stalin" simply stood for inspiration to freedom and justice, and had nothing to do with the horrible things which were "secretly" taking place in the Soviet Union. This excuse, of course, is all too slick and easy: one need not know the truth about the Stalinist terror in order to suspect that something was hideously wrong in Stalinism. Reading public texts–the official reports from the show trials, the attacks on enemies, the official panegyrics to Stalin and other leaders–should have been more than enough. In a way, everything one needs to know was already clear from these. This is why the truly surprising hypocrisy was the readiness of the Western communist observers to perceive the Stalinist accusations as a true psychological fact about the accused. In a letter to Walter Benjamin from 1938, Theodor Adorno reports a conversation he had with the left-leaning composer Hans Eisler in New York:

> I listened with not a little patience to his feeble defence of the Moscow trials, and with considerable disgust to the joke he cracked about the murder of Bukharin. He claims to have known the latter in Moscow, telling me that Bukharin's conscience was already so bad that he could not even look him, Eisler, honestly in the eyes.[9]

Eisler's psychological blindness is staggering here: he misreads Bukharin's terror–his fear of contact with foreigners when he knows that he is under observation and close to arrest–as an inner guilt feeling for the crimes he was accused of. How are we to understand this alongside the fact that the cultural products of high Stalinism were perceived by many in the West as the most authentic expression of authentic morality, one exuding a warm humanism and a faith in man (recall the reception in the West of Mark Donskoi's Gorky trilogy)? Perhaps one should move from reproaching the naivety of

Western fellow-travellers about the horrors of the
Stalinist Soviet Union to a more Deleuzian notion of a
contingent series intersecting and generating totally dis-
parate meanings, like a science-fiction story in which
scientists discover that the explosion which, in the Bible, signals the divine message, was effectively the vi-
sual trace of a terrible catastrophe that destroyed a
flourishing alien civilisation. That is to say, the difficult
thing to accept is that the horrors out of which the
Gorky trilogy grew in no way undermine the authenticity of its effect on a Western or even a Russian audi-
ence.

When the United Airlines Flight 93 and three other
planes were skyjacked on 9/11, it is significant that the
gist of the phone calls to their closest relatives from the
passengers who knew they were about to die was "I love
you." Martin Amis emphasised the Paulinian point that
all that ultimately matters is love: "Love is an abstract
noun, something nebulous. And yet love turns out to be
the only part of us that is solid, as the world turns up-
side down and the screen goes black."[10] However, a suspicion remains here: is this desperate confession of love
also not something of a sham, the same kind of fakery
as the sudden turn to God and prayer of someone who
suddenly faces the danger or proximity of death–a hypocritical opportunistic move born of fear, not of true
conviction? Why should there be more *truth* in what we
do in such desperate moments? Is it not rather that, in
such moments, the survival instinct makes us *betray our
desire*? In this sense, deathbed conversions or confessions of love are sacrifices of desire. According to numerous memoirs, many of the condemned at Stalinist

show trials faced the firing squad professing their innocence and their love for Stalin, a pathetic gesture aimed at redeeming their image in the eyes of the big Other. In this same vein, one cannot but be stricken by how, in their intimate correspondence, Ethel and Julius Rosenberg denied they were Soviet spies, playing innocent victims of an FBI plot, although, to the embarrassment of their defenders, recent documents prove that Julius at least was a spy (albeit a lower-level one than the prosecution claimed). The weird thing is that when one reads their intimate documents now, even knowing that he was indeed a spy, one still cannot escape the impression of utter sincerity, as if Rosenberg had convinced himself of his innocence. This fact becomes stranger still when one bears in mind that if he really believed in the Soviet Union, why, then, shouldn't he be spying for it, and be proud of it? (This, incidentally, brings us to what would have been a true ethical act: imagine a wife phoning her husband in the last seconds of her life to tell him: "Just wanted to let you know that our marriage was a sham, that I cannot stand the sight of you . . .")

Those Western leftists who heroically defied anti-communist hysteria in their own countries and did so with the utmost sincerity provide other instances of the tragic produced by the Cold War. They were prepared to go to prison for their communist convictions and in defence of the Soviet Union. Isn't it the very illusory nature of their belief that makes their subjective stance so tragically sublime? The miserable reality of the Stalinist Soviet Union gives their inner conviction a fragile beauty. This leads us to a radical and unexpected conclusion: it is not enough to say that we are dealing here with a tragically misplaced ethical conviction, with a blind trust that avoids confronting the miserable, terrifying reality of its ethical point of reference. What if, on the contrary, such a blindness, such a violent exclusionary gesture of refusing to see, such a disavowal of reality, such a fetishist attitude of "I know very well that things are horrible in the Soviet Union, but I believe none the less in Soviet socialism" is the innermost constituent of *every* ethical stance?

Kant was already well aware of this paradox when he deployed his notion of enthusiasm for the French Revolution in his *Conflict of Faculties* (1795). The Revolution's true significance does not reside in what actually went on in Paris–much of which was terrifying and included outbursts of murderous passion–but in the enthusiastic response that the events in Paris generated in the eyes of sympathetic observers all around Europe:

> The recent Revolution of a people which is rich in spirit, may well either fail or succeed, accumulate misery and atrocity, but nevertheless arouses in the heart of all spectators (who are not themselves caught up in it) a taking of sides according to desires [*eine Teilnehmung dem Wunsche nach*] which borders on enthusiasm and which, since its very expression was not without danger, can only have been caused by a moral disposition within the human race.[11]

To translate this into Lacanian language, the real event, the very dimension of the Real, was not in the immediate reality of the violent events in Paris, but in how this reality appeared to observers and in the hopes thus awakened in them. The reality of what went on in Paris belongs to the temporal dimension of empirical history; the sublime image that generated enthusiasm belongs to eternity . . .

Mutatis mutandis, the same applies for the Western admirers of the Soviet Union. The Soviet experience of "building socialism in one country" certainly did "accumulate misery and atrocity," but it nevertheless aroused enthusiasm in the heart of the spectators (who were not themselves caught up in it) . . . The question here is: does *every* ethics have to rely on such a gesture of fetishist disavowal? Is even the most universal ethics not obliged to draw a line and ignore some sort of suffering? What about animals slaughtered for our consumption? Who among us would be able to continue eating pork chops after visiting a factory farm in which pigs are half-blind and cannot even properly walk, but are just fattened to be killed? And what about, say, torture and suffering of millions we know about, but choose to ignore? Imagine the effect of having to watch a snuff movie portraying what goes on thousands of times a day around the world: brutal acts of torture, the picking out of eyes, the crushing of testicles–the list cannot bear recounting. Would the watcher be able to continue going on as usual? Yes, but only if he or she were able somehow to forget–in an act which suspended symbolic efficiency–what had been witnessed. This forgetting entails a gesture of what is called fetishist disavowal: "I know, but I don't want to know that I know, so I don't know." I know it, but I refuse to fully assume the consequences of this knowledge, so that I can continue acting as if I don't know it.

It begins to come clear that every ethics may well

have to rely on just this gesture of fetishist disavowal. Even the apparently obvious exception, the Buddhist ethics of solidarity with every living being, falls into this picture. After all, what Buddhism offers as a solution is a universalised indifference–a learning of how to withdraw from too much empathy. This is why Buddhism can so easily turn into the very opposite of universal compassion: the advocacy of a ruthless military attitude, which is what the fate of Zen Buddhism aptly demonstrates.

To wonder at this fact is not a proper philosophical attitude. That is to say, what if that which appears as an inconsistency, as the failure to draw all the consequences from one's ethical attitude, is, on the contrary, its positive condition of possibility? What if such an exclusion of some form of otherness from the scope of our ethical concerns is consubstantial with the very founding gesture of ethical universality, so that the more universal our explicit ethics is, the more brutal the underlying exclusion is? What the Christian all-inclusive attitude (recall St. Paul's famous "there are no men or women, no Jews and Greeks") involves is a thorough exclusion of those who do not accept inclusion into the Christian community. In other "particularistic" religions (and even in Islam, in spite of its global expansionism), there is a place for others: they are tolerated, even if they are looked upon with condescension. The Christian motto "All men are brothers," however, also means that those who do not accept brotherhood *are not men*. In the early years of the Iranian revolution, Khomeini played on the same paradox when he claimed, in an interview for the Western press, that the Iranian revolution was the most humane in all of history: not a single person was killed by the revolutionaries. When the surprised journalist asked about the death penalties publicised in the media, Khomeini calmly replied: "Those that we killed were not men, but criminal dogs!"

Christians usually praise themselves for overcoming the Jewish exclusivist notion of the Chosen People and encompassing the entirety of humanity. The catch is that, in their very insistence that they are the Chosen People with a privileged direct link to God, Jews accept the humanity of the other people who celebrate their false gods, while Christian universalism tendentiously excludes non-believers from the very universality of humankind.

So what about the opposite gesture–such as that made by the French philosopher Emmanuel Levinas–of abandoning the claim to sameness that underlies universality, and replacing it by a respect for otherness? There is, as Sloterdijk has pointed out, another obverse and much more unsettling dimension to the Levinasian figure of the Neighbour as the imponderable Other who deserves our unconditional respect.[12] That is, the imponderable Other as enemy, the enemy who is the absolute Other and no longer the "honourable enemy," but someone whose very reasoning is foreign to us, so that no authentic encounter with him in battle is possible. Although Levinas did not have this dimension in mind, the radical ambiguity, the traumatic character of the Neighbour makes it easy to understand how Levinas's notion of the Other prepared the ground (opened up the space) for it in a way strictly homologous to the way that Kantian ethics prepared the ground for the notion of diabolical evil. Horrible as it may sound, the Levinasian

Other as the abyss of otherness from which the ethical injunction emanates and the Nazi figure of the Jew as the less-than-human Other-enemy originate from the same source.

When Freud and Lacan insist on the problematic nature of the basic Judeo-Christian injunction to "love thy neighbour," they are thus not just making the standard critico-ideological point about how every notion of universality is coloured by our particular values and thus implies secret exclusions; they are making a much stronger point on the incompatibility of the Neighbour with the very dimension of universality. What resists universality is the properly *inhuman* dimension of the Neighbour. It is for this reason that finding oneself in the position of the beloved is so violent, traumatic even: being loved makes me feel directly the gap between what I am as a determinate being and the unfathomable X in me which causes love. Lacan's definition of love ("Love is giving something one doesn't have . . .") has to be supplemented with: ". . . to someone who doesn't want it." Indeed, are we aware that Yeats's well-known lines describe one of the most claustrophobic constellations that one can imagine?

Had I the heavens' embroidered cloths,
Enwrought with golden and silver light,
The blue and the dim and the dark cloths
Of night and light and the half-light,
I would spread the cloths under your feet:
But I, being poor, have only my dreams;
I have spread my dreams under your feet,
Tread softly because you tread on my dreams.

In short, as the French philosopher Gilles Deleuze put it, *"Si vous êtes pris dans le rêve de l'autre, vous êtez foutu"* (If you're trapped in the dream of the other, you're fucked!); or, as Neil Gaiman, the author of the graphic novel *The Sandman*, wrote in a memorable passage:

> Have you ever been in love? Horrible isn't it? It makes you so vulnerable. It opens your chest and it opens up your heart and it means that someone can get inside you and mess you up. You build up all these defenses, you build up a whole suit of armor, so that nothing can hurt you, then one stupid person, no different from any other stupid person, wanders into your stupid life . . . You give them a piece of you. They didn't ask for it. They did something dumb one day, like kiss you or smile at you, and then your life isn't your own anymore. Love takes hostages. It gets inside you. It eats you out and leaves you crying in the darkness, so simple a phrase like "maybe we should be just friends" turns into a glass splinter working its way into your heart. It hurts. Not just in the imagination. Not just in the mind. It's a soul-hurt, a real gets-inside-you-and-rips-you-apart pain. I hate love.[13]

In the last years of his life, Soviet film director Andrei Tarkovsky lived in Stockholm, working on *The Sacrifice*. He was given an office in the same building in which Ingmar Bergman, who at that time still lived in Stockholm, had his. Although the two directors had deep respect and supreme mutual admiration, they never met, but carefully avoided each other, as if their direct encounter would have been too painful and doomed to fail on account of the very proximity of their universes. They invented and respected their own code of discretion.

The Violence of Language

So why, today, this fear of the over-proximity of the Other as subject of desire? Why the need to decaffeinate the Other, to deprive him or her of their raw substance of *jouissance*? I suspect this is a reaction to the disintegration of the protective symbolic walls that kept others at a proper distance. What we lack in our culture, where brutal self-confessions are countered by the politically correct fear of harassment which keeps the Other at bay, is the spirit best expressed by Gore Vidal. Vidal gave the perfect answer to a vulgarly intrusive journalist who had asked him point-blank whether his first sexual partner was a man or a woman: "I was too polite to ask," he said.

Nowhere is this disintegration of the protective walls of civility more palpable than in the clashes of different cultures. In the autumn of 2005, the West was captivated by an explosion of violence which threatened to spill over into a literal clash of civilisations: the widespread demonstrations in Arab countries against caricatures of the Prophet Muhammad published in *Jyllands-Posten*, a small-circulation Danish newspaper. The first thing to be noted, so obvious that as a rule it's overlooked, is that the vast majority of the thousands who felt offended by and demonstrated against the cartoons had not even *seen* them. This fact confronts us with another, less attractive, aspect of globalisation: the "global information village" is the condition of the fact that something which appeared in an obscure daily in Denmark caused a violent stir in distant Muslim countries. It is as if Denmark and Syria,

Pakistan, Egypt, Iraq, Lebanon, and Indonesia really were *neighbouring* countries. Those who understand globalisation as an opportunity for the entire earth to be a unified space of communication, one which brings together all humanity, often fail to notice this dark side of their proposition. Since a Neighbour is, as Freud suspected long ago, primarily a thing, a traumatic intruder, someone whose different way of life (or rather, way of *jouissance* materialised in its social practices and rituals) disturbs us, throws the balance of our way of life off the rails, when it comes too close, this can also give rise to an aggressive reaction aimed at getting rid of this disturbing intruder. As Peter Sloterdijk put it: "More communication means at first above all more conflict."[14] This is why he is right to claim that the attitude of "understanding-each-other" has to be supplemented by the attitude of "getting-out-of-each-other's-way," by maintaining an appropriate distance, by implementing a new "code of discretion."

European civilisation finds it easier to tolerate different ways of life precisely on account of what its critics usually denounce as its weakness and failure, namely the alienation of social life. One of the things alienation means is that distance is woven into the very social texture of everyday life. Even if I live side by side with others, in my normal state I ignore them. I am allowed not to get too close to others. I move in a social space where I interact with others obeying certain external "mechanical" rules, without sharing their inner world. Perhaps the lesson to be learned is that sometimes a dose of alienation is indispensable for peaceful coexistence. Sometimes alienation is not a problem but a solution.

The Muslim crowds did not react to the Muhammad caricatures as such. They reacted to the complex figure or image of the *West* that they perceived as the attitude behind the caricatures. Those who propose the term "Occidentalism" as the counterpart to Edward Said's "Orientalism" are right up to a point: what we get in Muslim countries is a certain ideological vision of the West which distorts Western reality no less, although in a different way, than the Orientalist vision distorts the Orient. What exploded in violence was a web of symbols, images, and attitudes, including Western imperialism, godless materialism, hedonism, and the suffering of Palestinians, and which became attached to the Danish cartoons. This is why the hatred expanded from the caricatures to Denmark as a country, to Scandinavia, to Europe, and to the West as a whole. A torrent of humiliations and frustrations were condensed into the caricatures. This condensation, it needs to be borne in mind, is a basic fact of language, of constructing and imposing a certain symbolic field.

This simple and all too obvious reflection on the way in which language works renders problematic the prevalent idea of language and the symbolic order as the medium of reconciliation and mediation, of peaceful coexistence, as opposed to a violent medium of immediate and raw confrontation.[15] In language, instead of exerting direct violence on each other, we are meant to debate, to exchange words, and such an exchange, even when it is aggressive, presupposes a minimal recognition of the other party. The entry into language and the renunciation of violence are often understood as two aspects of one and the same gesture: "Speaking is the foundation and structure of socialization, and happens to be characterized by the renunciation of violence," as a text by Jean-Marie Muller written for UNESCO tells us.[16] Since man is a "speaking animal," this means that the renunciation of violence defines the very core of being human: "it is actually the principles and methods of non-violence . . . that constitute the humanity of human beings, the coherence and relevance of moral standards based both on convictions and a sense of responsibility," so that violence is "indeed a radical perversion of humanity."[17] Insofar as language gets infected by violence, this occurs under the influence of contingent "pathological" circumstances which distort the inherent logic of symbolic communication.

What if, however, humans exceed animals in their capacity for violence precisely because they *speak*?[18] As Hegel was already well aware, there is something violent in the very symbolisation of a thing, which equals its mortification. This violence operates at multiple levels. Language simplifies the designated thing, reducing it to a single feature. It dismembers the thing, destroying its organic unity, treating its parts and properties as autonomous. It inserts the thing into a field of meaning which is ultimately external to it. When we name gold "gold," we violently extract a metal from its natural texture, investing into it our dreams of wealth, power, spiritual purity, and so on, which have nothing whatsoever to do with the immediate reality of gold.

Lacan condensed this aspect of language in his notion of the Master-Signifier which "quilts" and thus holds together a symbolic field. That is to say, for Lacan–at least for his theory of four discourses elaborated in the late 1960s[19]–human communication in its most basic, constitutive dimension does not involve a space of egalitarian intersubjectivity. It is not "balanced." It does not put the participants in symmetric mutually responsible positions where they all have to follow the same rules and justify their claims with reasons. On the contrary, what Lacan indicates with his notion of the discourse of the Master as the first (inaugural, constitutive) form of discourse is that every concrete, "really existing" space of discourse is ultimately grounded in a violent imposition of a Master-Signifier which is *stricto sensu* "irrational": it cannot be further grounded in reasons. It is the point at which one can only say that "the buck stops here"; a point at which, in order to stop the endless regress, somebody has to say, *"It is so because I say it is so!"* Here, Levinas was right to emphasise the fundamentally asymmetrical character of intersubjectivity: there is never a balanced reciprocity in my encountering another subject. The appearance of *égalité* is always discursively sustained by an asymmetric axis of master versus servant, of the bearer of university knowledge versus its object, of a pervert versus a hysteric, and so on. This, of course, runs against the predominant ideological approach to the topic of violence which understands it as "spontaneous," an approach well exemplified in Muller's text for UNESCO, which acquired a semi-official programmatic status.[20] Muller's starting point is the rejection of all attempts to distinguish between "good" and "bad" violence:

> It is essential to define violence in such a way that it cannot be qualified as "good." The moment we claim to

be able to distinguish "good" violence from "bad," we lose the proper use of the word, and get into a muddle. Above all, as soon as we claim to be developing criteria by which to define a supposedly "good" violence, each of us will find it easy to make use of these in order to justify our own acts of violence.

But how can one wholly repudiate violence when struggle and aggression are part of life? The easy way out is a terminological distinction between the "aggression" that effectively amounts to a "life-force" and the "violence" that is a "death-force": "violence," here, is not aggression as such, but its excess, which disturbs the normal run of things by desiring always more and more. The task becomes to get rid of this excess.

Desiring property and power is legitimate insofar as it enables an individual to achieve independence from others. Adversaries in a conflict, however, each have a natural tendency always to demand more. Nothing is enough for them, and they are never satisfied. They do not know how to stop themselves; they know no limits. Desire demands more, much more, than need. "There is always a sense of limitlessness in desire,"[21] wrote the French religious thinker Simone Weil. To begin with, individuals seek power so as not to be dominated by others. But if they are not careful, they can soon find themselves overstepping the limit beyond which they are actually seeking to dominate others. Rivalry between human beings can only be surmounted when each individual puts a limit on his or her own desires. "Limited desires," notes Weil, "are in harmony with the world; desires that contain the infinite are not."[22]

This approach remains firmly within premodern Aristotelian coordinates: the task is to retain the proper measure in desiring. Modernity is, however, defined by the coordinates of the Kantian philosophical revolution, in which *the absolute excess is that of the law itself*. The law intervenes in the "homogeneous" stability of our pleasure-oriented life as the shattering force of an absolute destabilising "heterogeneity." G. K. Chesterton made the same point in his famous "Defence of Detective Stories," in which he remarks how the detective story:

> keeps in some sense before the mind the fact that civilisation itself is the most sensational of departures and the most romantic of rebellions . . . It is the agent of social justice who is the original and poetic figure, while the burglars and footpads are merely placid old cosmic conservatives, happy in the immemorial respectability of apes and wolves. [The police romance] is based on the fact that morality is the most dark and daring of conspiracies.[23]

There is the elementary matrix of the Hegelian dialectical process here: the external opposition (between law and its criminal transgression) is transformed into the opposition, internal to the transgression itself, between particular transgressions and the absolute transgression which appears as its opposite, as the universal law. And *mutatis mutandis,* the same goes for violence: when we perceive something as an act of violence, we measure it by a presupposed standard of what the "normal" non-violent situation is–and the highest form of violence is the imposition of this standard with reference to which some events appear as "violent." This is why language itself, the very medium of non-violence, of mutual recognition, involves unconditional violence. In other words, it is language itself which pushes our desire beyond proper limits, transforming it into a "desire that contains the infinite," elevating it into an absolute striving that cannot ever be satisfied. What Lacan calls *objet petit a* is precisely this ethereal "undead" object, the surplus object that causes desire in its excessive and derailing aspect. One cannot get rid of this excess: it is consubstantial with human desire as such.

So, to paraphrase Weil, in modernity, "limited desires in harmony with the world" are the ultimate source of our opportunist anti-ethical stance, they sustain the inertia of egotism and pleasure-seeking, while our contact with the good is sustained by "desires that contain the infinite," that strive for the absolute. This gives rise to an irreducible ambiguity: the source of the good is a power that shatters the coordinates of our finite existence, a destructive power that, from the standpoint of our limited stable life-form, cannot but appear as evil. The same goes for the relationship between mortality and immortality. According to the traditional ideological commonplace, immortality is linked to the good and mortality to evil: what makes us good is the awareness of immortality (of God, of our soul, of the sublime ethical striving . . .), while the root of evil is the resignation to our mortality (we shall all die, so it doesn't really matter, just grab what you can, indulge your darkest whims . . .). What, however, if one turns this commonplace round and wages the hypothesis that the primordial immortality is that of evil: evil is something which threatens to return for ever, a spectral dimension which magically survives its physical annihilation and continues to haunt us. This is why the victory of good over evil is the ability to die, to regain the innocence of nature, to find peace in getting rid of the obscene infinity of evil. Recall the classical scene from old horror movies: when a man who was possessed by some evil force–this possession being signalled by a freakish disfiguration of the body–is delivered from the undead spectre that colonised him, he regains the serene beauty of his everyday form and dies in peace. This is why Christ has to die–pagan gods who cannot die are embodiments of obscene evil. Good versus evil is not spirit versus nature: the primordial evil is spirit itself with its violent derailment of nature. The conclusion to be drawn from this is that the properly human good, the good elevated above the natural good, the infinite spiritual good, is ultimately *the mask of evil*.

So, perhaps, the fact that *reason* and *race* have the same root in Latin (*ratio*) tells us something: language, not primitive egotistic interest, is the first and greatest divider, it is because of language that we and our neighbours (can) "live in different worlds" even when we live on the same street. What this means is that verbal violence is not a secondary distortion, but the ultimate resort of every specifically human violence. Take the example of anti-Semitic pogroms, which can stand in for all racist violence. What the perpetrators of pogroms find intolerable and rage-provoking, what they react to, is not the immediate reality of Jews, but the image/figure of the "Jew" which circulates and has been constructed in their tradition. The catch, of course, is that one single individual cannot distinguish in any simple way between real

Jews and their anti-Semitic image: this image overdeter-
mines the way I experience real Jews themselves, and
furthermore it affects the way Jews experience themselves. What makes a real Jew that an anti-Semite encounters on the street "intolerable," what the anti-Semite
tries to destroy when he attacks the Jew, the true target of
his fury, is this fantasmatic dimension.

The same principle applies to every political protest:
when workers protest their exploitation, they do not
protest a simple reality, but an experience of their real
predicament made meaningful through language. Reality in itself, in its stupid existence, is never intolerable:
it is language, its symbolisation, which makes it such.
So precisely when we are dealing with the scene of a
furious crowd, attacking and burning buildings and
cars, lynching people, etc., we should never forget the
placards they are carrying and the words which sustain
and justify their acts. It was Heidegger who elaborated
this feature at the formal-ontological level when, in his
reading of "essence or *Wesen*" as a verb ("essencing"),
he provided a de-essentialised notion of essence. Traditionally, "essence" refers to a stable core that guarantees
the identity of a thing. For Heidegger, "essence" is something that depends on the historical context, on the ep-
ochal disclosure of being that occurs in and through
language. He calls this the "house of being." His expression "*Wesen der Sprache*" does not mean "the essence of
language," but the "essencing," the making of essences,
that is the work of language:

> [. . .] language bringing things into their essence,
> language "moving us" so that things matter to us in a

> particular kind of way, so that paths are made within
> which we can move among entities, and so that entities
> can bear on each other as the entities they are ... We
> share an originary language when the world is
> articulated in the same style for us, when we "listen to
> language," when we "let it say its saying to us."[24]

Let's unravel this a little. For a medieval Christian, the "essence" of gold resides in its incorruptibility and divine sheen which make it a "divine" metal. For us, it is either a flexible resource to be used for industrial purposes or a material appropriate for aesthetic purposes. Another example: the castrato voice was once the very voice of angels prior to the Fall; for us today, it is a monstrous creation. This change in our sensitivity is sustained by language; it hinges on the shift in our symbolic universe. A fundamental violence exists in this "essencing" ability of language: our world is given a partial twist, it loses its balanced innocence, one partial colour gives the tone of the whole. The operation designated by the political thinker Ernesto Laclau as that of hegemony is inherent to language. So when, in his reading of the famous chorus from *Antigone* on the "uncanny/demonic" character of man in the *Introduction to Metaphysics,* Heidegger deploys the notion of "ontological" violence that pertains to every founding gesture of the new communal world of a people, accomplished by poets, thinkers, and statesmen, one should always bear in mind that this "uncanny/demonic" dimension is ultimately that of language itself:

> Violence is usually seen in terms of the domain in which
> concurring compromise and mutual assistance set the

standard for *Dasein,* and accordingly all violence is necessarily deemed only a disturbance and an offence . . . The violent one, the creative one who sets forth into the unsaid, who breaks into the unthought, who compels what has never happened and makes appear what is unseen–this violent one stands at all times in daring . . . Therefore the violence-doer knows no kindness and conciliation (in the ordinary sense), no appeasement and mollification by success or prestige and by their confirmation . . . For such a one, disaster is the deepest and broadest Yes to the Overwhelming . . . Essential de-cision, when it is carried out and when it resists the constantly pressing ensnarement in the everyday and the customary, has to use violence. This act of violence, this de-cided setting out upon the way to the Being of beings, moves humanity out of the hominess of what is most directly nearby and what is usual.[25]

As such, the Creator is "*hupsipolis apolis*" (*Antigone,* line 370): he stands outside and above *polis* and its *ethos*; he is unbound by any rules of "morality" (which are only a degenerative form of *ethos*); only as such can he ground a new form of *ethos,* of communal being in a *polis* . . . Of course, what reverberates here is the topic of an "illegal" violence that founds the rule of the law it-self.[26] Heidegger hastens to add how the first victim of this violence is the Creator himself, who has to be erased with the advent of the new order that he grounded. This erasure can take different forms. The first is physical destruction–from Moses and Julius Caesar onwards, we know that a founding figure has to be killed. But there is also the relapse into madness, as in the case of great poets, from Hölderlin to Ezra Pound, who were blinded by the very force of their poetic vision. Interestingly, the point in *Antigone* where the chorus bewails man as the most "demonic" of all creatures, as a being of excess, a being who violates all proper measures, comes immediately after it is revealed that someone has defied Creon's order and performed the funeral ritual on Polyneices body.[27] It is *this* act which is perceived as a "demonic" excessive act, not Creon's prohibition. Antigone is far from being the place-holder of moderation, of respect for proper limits, against Creon's sacrilegious hubris; quite the contrary, the true violence is hers.

What accounts for the chilling character of the quoted passage is that Heidegger does not merely provide a new variation on his standard rhetorical figure of inversion ("the essence of violence has nothing to do with ontic violence, suffering, war, destruction, etc.; the essence of violence resides in the violent character of the very imposition/founding of the new mode of the Essence–disclosure of communal Being–itself"); implicitly, but clearly, Heidegger reads this essential violence as something that grounds–or at least opens up the space for–the explosions of ontic or physical violence itself. Consequently, we should not immunise ourselves against the effects of the violence Heidegger is talking about by classifying it as "merely" ontological: although it is violent as such, imposing a certain disclosure of world, this world constellation also involves social relations of authority. In his interpretation of Heraclitus fragment 53 ("Conflict [*polemos*] is the father of all things and king of all. Some he shows to be gods and others men; some he makes slaves and others free"),

Heidegger–in contrast to those who accuse him of omitting to consider the "cruel" aspects of the ancient Greek life (slavery, etc.)–openly draws attention to how "rank and dominance" are directly grounded in a disclosure of being, thereby providing a direct ontological grounding to social relations of domination:

> If people today from time to time are going to busy themselves rather too eagerly with the polis of the Greeks, they should not suppress this side of it; otherwise the concept of the polis easily becomes innocuous and sentimental. What is higher in rank is what is stronger. Thus Being, logos, as the gathered harmony, is not easily available for every man at the same price, but is concealed, as opposed to that harmony which is always mere equalizing, the elimination of tension, leveling.[28]

There is thus a direct link between the ontological violence and the texture of social violence (of sustaining relations of enforced domination) that pertains to language. In her *America Day by Day* (1948), Simone de Beauvoir noted: "many racists, ignoring the rigors of science, insist on declaring that even if the psychological reasons haven't been established, the fact is that blacks *are* inferior. You only have to travel through America to be convinced of it."[29] Her point about racism has been too easily misunderstood. In a recent commentary, for example, Stella Sandford claims that "nothing justifies Beauvoir's . . . acceptance of the 'fact' of this inferiority":

> With her existentialist philosophical framework, we might rather have expected Beauvoir to talk about the

> *interpretation of* existing physiological differences in
> terms of inferiority and superiority . . . or to point out
> the mistake involved in the use of the value judgements
> "inferior" and "superior" to name alleged properties of
> human beings, as if to "confirm a given fact."[30]

It is clear what bothers Sandford here. She is aware that
Beauvoir's claim about the factual inferiority of blacks
aims at something more than the simple social fact that,
in the American South of (not only) that time, blacks
were treated as inferior by the white majority and, in a
way, they effectively *were* inferior. But her critical solution, propelled by the care to avoid racist claims on the
factual inferiority of blacks, is to relativise their inferiority into a matter of interpretation and judgment by
white racists, and distance it from a question of their
very being. But what this softening distinction misses is
the truly trenchant dimension of racism: the "being" of
blacks (as of whites or anyone else) is a socio-symbolic
being. When they are treated by whites as inferior, this
does indeed make them inferior at the level of their
socio-symbolic identity. In other words, the white racist
ideology exerts a performative efficiency. It is not merely
an interpretation of what blacks are, but an interpretation that determines the very being and social existence
of the interpreted subjects.

We can now locate precisely what makes Sandford
and other critics of Beauvoir resist her formulation that
blacks actually *were* inferior: this resistance is itself ideological. At the base of this ideology is the fear that, if
one concedes this point, we will have lost the inner freedom, autonomy, and dignity of the human individual.

Which is why such critics insist that blacks are not inferior but merely "inferiorised" by the violence imposed on them by white racist discourse. That is, they are affected by an imposition which does not affect them in the very core of their being, and consequently which they can (and do) resist as free autonomous agents through their acts, dreams, and projects.

This brings us back to the starting point of this chapter, the abyss of the Neighbour. Though it may appear that there is a contradiction between the way discourse constitutes the very core of the subject's identity and the notion of this core as an unfathomable abyss beyond the "wall of language," there is a simple solution to this apparent paradox. The "wall of language" which forever separates me from the abyss of another subject is simultaneously that which opens up and sustains this abyss–the very obstacle that separates me from the Beyond is what creates its mirage.

Andante ma non troppo e molto cantabile

"A BLOOD-DIMMED TIDE IS LOOSED"

A Strange Case of Phatic Communication

The French suburban riots of autumn 2005 saw thousands of cars burning and a major outburst of public violence. Parallels were often drawn with the New Orleans looting after hurricane Katrina hit the city on 29 August 2005 and with the May '68 events in Paris. In spite of significant differences, lessons can be drawn from both parallels. The Paris fires had a sobering effect on those European intellectuals who had used New Orleans to emphasise the advantage of the European welfare state model over the wild capitalism of the U.S.: now it was clear, such things could happen in welfare France, too. Those who had attributed the New Orleans violence to the lack of European-style solidarity were proved no less wrong than the U.S. free-market liberals, who now gleefully returned the blow and pointed out how the very rigidity of state interventions which limit market competition and its dynamics prevented the economic rise of the marginalised immigrants in France–in contrast to the U.S. where many immigrant groups are among the most successful.

The parallels with May '68 make clear the total absence of any positive utopian prospect among the protesters: if May '68 was a revolt with a utopian vision, the 2005 revolt was just an outburst with no pretence to vision. If the much-repeated commonplace that we live in a post-ideological era has any sense, it is here. There were no particular demands made by the protesters in the Paris suburbs. There was only an insistence on *recognition,* based on a vague, unarticulated *ressentiment*. Most of those interviewed talked about how unacceptable it was that the then interior minister, Nicolas Sarkozy, had called them "scum." In a weird self-referential short-circuit, they were protesting against the very reaction to their protests. "Populist reason" here encounters its irrational limit: what we have is a zero-level protest, a violent protest act which demands nothing. There was an irony in watching the sociologists, intellectuals, and commentators trying to understand and help. Desperately they tried to discern the meaning of the protesters' actions: "We must do something about the integration of immigrants, about their welfare, their job opportunities," they proclaimed–in the process they obfuscated the key enigma the riots presented.

The protesters, although effectively underprivileged and de facto excluded, were in no way living on the edge of starvation. Nor had they been reduced to the level of bare survival. People in much worse material straits, let alone conditions of physical and ideological oppression, had been able to organise themselves into political agencies with clear or even fuzzy agendas. The fact that there was *no* programme behind the burning Paris suburbs is thus itself a fact to be interpreted. It tells us a great deal about our ideologico-political predicament. What kind of universe is it that we inhabit, which can celebrate itself as a society of choice, but in which the only option available to enforced democratic consensus is a blind acting out? The sad fact that opposition to the system cannot articulate itself in the guise of a realistic alternative, or at least a meaningful utopian project, but only take the shape of a meaningless outburst, is a grave illustration of our predicament. What does our celebrated freedom of choice serve, when the only choice is between playing by the rules and (self-)destructive violence? The protesters' violence was almost exclusively directed against their own. The cars burned and the schools torched were not those of richer neighbourhoods. They were part of the hard-won acquisitions of the very strata from which the protesters originated.

What needs to be resisted when faced with the shocking reports and images of the burning Paris suburbs is what I call the hermeneutic temptation: the search for some deeper meaning or message hidden in these outbursts. What is most difficult to accept is precisely the riots' meaninglessness: more than a form of protest, they are what Lacan called a *passage a l'acte*–an impulsive movement into action which can't be translated into speech or thought and carries with it an intolerable weight of frustration. This bears witness not only to the impotence of the perpetrators, but, even more, to the lack of what cultural analyst Fredric Jameson has called "cognitive mapping," an inability to locate the experience of their situation within a meaningful whole.

The Paris outbursts were thus not rooted in any kind of concrete socio-economic protest, still less in an assertion of Islamic fundamentalism. One of the first sites to be burned was a mosque–which is why the Muslim religious bodies immediately condemned the violence.

The riots were simply a direct effort to gain *visibility*. A social group which, although part of France and composed of French citizens, saw itself as excluded from the political and social space proper wanted to render its presence palpable to the general public. Their actions spoke for them: like it or not, we're here, no matter how much you pretend not to see us. Commentators failed to notice the crucial fact that the protesters did not claim any special status for themselves as members of a religious or ethnic community striving for its self-enclosed way of life. On the contrary, their main premise was that they wanted to be and *were* French citizens, but were not fully recognised as such.

The French philosopher Alain Finkielkraut created a scandal in France when, in an interview for the Israeli newspaper *Ha'aretz*, he qualified the riots as an "anti-republican pogrom" and "an ethnic-religious revolt." He was missing the point: the message of the outbursts was not that the protesters found their ethnic-religious identity threatened by French republican universalism but, on the contrary, that they were not included in it, that they found themselves on the other side of the wall which separates the visible from the invisible part of the republican social space. They were neither offering a solution nor constituting a movement for providing a solution. Their aim was to create a problem, to signal that they were a problem that could no longer be ignored. This is why violence was necessary. Had they organised a non-violent march, all they would have got was a small note on the bottom of a page . . .

The fact that the violent protesters wanted and demanded to be recognised as full French citizens, of course, signals not only the failure to integrate them, but simultaneously the crisis of the French model of integration into citizenship, with its implicitly racist exclusionary normativeness. Within the space of French state ideology, the term "citizen" is opposed to "indigene," and suggests a primitive part of the population not yet mature enough to deserve full citizenship. This is why the protesters' demand to be recognised also implies a rejection of the very framework through which recognition takes place. It is a call for the construction of a new universal framework.[1]

This brings us once more to our point of departure: the story about the worker stealing wheelbarrows. Analysts who were searching the wheelbarrows for their content and the riots for their hidden meaning were missing the obvious. As Marshall McLuhan would have put it, here the medium itself was the message.

In the golden era of structuralism, Roman Jakobson deployed the notion of "phatic" function, which he derived from Malinowski's concept of phatic communion, the use of language to maintain a social relation through ritualised formulas such as greetings, chit-chat about the weather, and related formal niceties of social communication. A good structuralist, Jakobson included the means of discontinuing communication: as he put it, the mere purport of prolonging communicative contact suggests the emptiness of such contact. He quotes a dialogue from Dorothy Parker:

"Well, here we are," he said.
"Here we are," she said, "Aren't we?"
"I should say we are," he said.

The emptiness of contact thus has a propitious technical function as a test of the system itself: a "Hello, do you hear me?" The phatic function is therefore close to the "meta-linguistic" function: it checks whether the channel is working. Simultaneously, the addresser and the addressee check whether they are using the same code.[2] Is this not exactly what took place in the violent outbursts in the Paris suburbs? Was the basic message not a kind of "Hello, do you hear me?," a testing both of the channel and of the code itself?

Alain Badiou has reflected that we live in a social space which is progressively experienced as "worldless."[3] In such a space, the only form protest can take is "meaningless" violence. Even Nazi anti-Semitism, however ghastly it was, opened up a world: it described its present critical situation by positing an enemy which was a "Jewish conspiracy"; it named a goal and the means of achieving it. Nazism disclosed reality in a way which allowed its subjects to acquire a global "cognitive mapping," which included a space for their meaningful engagement. Perhaps it is here that one of the main dangers of capitalism should be located: although it is global and encompasses the whole world, it sustains a *stricto sensu* "worldless" ideological constellation, depriving the large majority of people of any meaningful cognitive mapping. Capitalism is the first socio-economic order which *detotalises meaning*: it is not global at the level of meaning (there is no global "capitalist worldview," no "capitalist civilisation" proper–the fundamental lesson of globalisation is precisely that capitalism can accommodate itself to all civilisations, from Christian to Hindu or Buddhist, from West to East); its global dimension can only be formulated at the level of truth-without-meaning, as the "Real" of the global market mechanism.

The first conclusion to be drawn from the French riots is thus that both conservative and liberal reactions to the unrest clearly fail. The conservatives emphasise the clash of civilisations and, predictably, law and order. Immigrants should not abuse our hospitality. They are our guests, so they should respect our customs. Our society has the right to safeguard its unique culture and way of life. There is no excuse for crime and violent behaviour. What young immigrants need is not more social help, but discipline and hard work . . . Meanwhile leftist liberals, no less predictably, stick to their mantra about neglected social programmes and integration efforts, which have deprived the younger generation of immigrants of any clear economic and social prospects: violent outbursts are their only way to articulate their dissatisfaction. As Stalin might have said, it is meaningless debating which reaction is worse: they are *both* worse, and that includes the warning formulated by both sides about the real danger of these outbursts residing in the easily predictable racist *reaction* of the French populace itself.

The Paris riots need to be situated in a series they form with another type of violence that the liberal majority today perceives as a threat to our way of life: direct terrorist attacks and suicide bombings. In both instances, violence and counter-violence are caught up in a deadly vicious cycle, each generating the very forces it tries to combat. In both cases we are dealing with blind *passages a l'acte,* where violence is an implicit admission of impotence. The difference is that, in contrast to the Paris outbursts, which were a zero-level protest, a violent outburst which wanted nothing, terrorist attacks are carried out on behalf of that *absolute* meaning provided by religion. Their ultimate target is the entire Western godless way of life based on modern science. Science today effectively does compete with religion, insofar as it serves two properly *ideological* needs, those for hope and those for censorship, which were traditionally taken care of by religion. To quote John Gray:

> Science alone has the power to silence heretics. Today it is the only institution that can claim authority. Like the Church in the past, it has the power to destroy, or marginalize, independent thinkers . . . From the standpoint of anyone who values freedom of thought, this may be unfortunate, but it is undoubtedly the chief source of science's appeal. For us, science is a refuge from uncertainties, promising–and in some measure delivering–the miracle of freedom from thought, while churches have become sanctuaries for doubt.[4]

We are not talking here about science as such, so the idea of science sustaining "freedom from thought" is not a variation on Heidegger's notion that "science doesn't think." We are talking about the way science functions as a social force, as an ideological institution: at this level, its function is to provide certainty, to be a point of reference on which one can rely, and to provide hope. New technological inventions will help us fight disease, prolong life, and so on. In this dimension, science is what Lacan called "university discourse" at its purest: knowledge whose "truth" is a Master-Signifier, that is, power.[5] Science and religion have changed places: today, science provides the security religion once guaranteed. In a curious inversion, religion is one of the possible places from which one can deploy critical doubts about today's society. It has become one of the sites of resistance.

The "worldless" character of capitalism is linked to this hegemonic role of the scientific discourse in modernity. Hegel had already clearly identified this feature when he noted that for us moderns, art and religion no longer command absolute respect: we can admire them, but we no longer kneel down before them, our heart is not really with them. Only science–conceptual knowledge–deserves this respect. And it is only psychoanalysis that can disclose the full contours of the shattering impact of modernity–that is, capitalism combined with the hegemony of scientific discourse–on the way our identity is grounded in symbolic identifications. No wonder modernity led to the so-called "crisis of sense," that is, to the disintegration of the link between, or even identity of, truth and meaning.

In Europe, where modernisation took place over several centuries, there was time to adjust to this break, to soften its shattering impact, through *Kulturarbeit*, the work of culture. New social narratives and myths slowly came into being. Some other societies–notably the Muslim ones–were exposed to this impact directly, without a protective screen or temporal delay, so their symbolic universe was perturbed much more brutally. They lost their (symbolic) ground with no time left to establish a new (symbolic) balance. No wonder, then, that the only way for some of these societies to avoid total breakdown was to erect in panic the shield of "fundamentalism," that psychotic-delirious-incestuous reassertion of religion as direct insight into the divine Real, with all the terrifying consequences that such a reassertion entails, and including the return with a vengeance of the obscene superego divinity demanding sacrifices.

As to the "terrorist" attacks by fundamentalists, the first thing that strikes the eye is the inadequacy of the idea, developed most systematically by Donald Davidson, that human acts are rationally intentional and accountable in terms of the beliefs and desires of the agent.[6] Such an approach exemplifies the racist bias of the theories of "rationality." Although their aim is to understand the Other from within, they end up attributing to the Other the most ridiculous beliefs–including the infamous 400 virgins awaiting the believer in paradise as a "rational" explanation of why he is ready to blow himself up. In their effort to make the Other "like us," they end up making him ridiculously weird.[7]

Here is a passage from one of the propaganda texts distributed by North Korea during the Korean War:

Hero Kang Ho-yung was seriously wounded in both arms and both legs in the Kamak Hill Battle, so he rolled into the midst of the enemy with a hand grenade in his mouth and wiped them out, shouting: "My arms and legs were broken. But on the contrary my retaliatory spirit against you scoundrels became a thousand times stronger. I will show the unbending fighting will of a member of the Workers' Party of Korea

and unflinching will firmly pledged to the Party and the
Leader!"[8]

It is easy to laugh at the ridiculously unrealistic character of this description: how could poor Kang talk if he
was holding the grenade with his mouth? And how is it
that, in the midst of a fierce battle, there was time for
such a long declamatory proclamation? However, what
if the mistake is to read this passage as a realistic description and thus impute ridiculous beliefs to Koreans? Asked directly, it is clear that North Koreans
would reply: of course this story is not literally true–it
is just meant to render the unconditional spirit of sacrifice and the readiness of the Korean people to do the
impossible in order to defeat the imperialist aggression
on their land . . . What if the mistake is the same as
that of the anthropologists who impute to "primitive"
aborigines celebrating the eagle as their ancestor the
belief that they are really descended from the eagle?
Why not read this passage–which effectively sounds
operatic in its pathos–in the way we might listen to Act
III of Wagner's *Tristan*, where the mortally wounded
hero sings his extremely demanding dying chant for
almost an hour? Which of us is ready to impute to
Wagner the belief that this is possible? But singing
Tristan's death is much more difficult than what the
unfortunate Kang did . . . Perhaps we should imagine
Kang singing an aria before rolling under the tank, in
that properly operatic moment of the suspension of the
flow of real time when, in a song, the hero reflects on
what he is about to do.

Terrorist Resentment

William Butler Yeats's "Second Coming" seems perfectly to render our present predicament: "The best lack all conviction, while the worst / Are full of passionate intensity." This is an excellent description of the current split between anaemic liberals and impassioned fundamentalists. "The best" are no longer able fully to engage, while "the worst" engage in racist, religious, sexist fanaticism.

However, are the terrorist fundamentalists, be they Christian or Muslim, really fundamentalists in the authentic sense of the term? Do they really believe? What they lack is a feature that is easy to discern in all authentic fundamentalists, from Tibetan Buddhists to the Amish in the U.S.: the absence of resentment and envy, the deep indifference towards the non-believers' way of life. If today's so-called fundamentalists really believe they have found their way to truth, why should they feel threatened by non-believers, why should they envy them? When a Buddhist encounters a Western hedonist, he hardly condemns him. He just benevolently notes that the hedonist's search for happiness is self-defeating. In contrast to true fundamentalists, the terrorist pseudo-fundamentalists are deeply bothered, intrigued, fascinated by the sinful life of the non-believers. One can feel that, in fighting the sinful Other, they are fighting their own temptation. These so-called Christian or Muslim fundamentalists are a disgrace to true fundamentalism.

It is here that Yeats's diagnosis falls short of the present predicament: the passionate intensity of a mob bears witness to a lack of true conviction. Deep in themselves, terrorist fundamentalists also lack true conviction–their violent outbursts are proof of it. How fragile the belief of a Muslim must be, if he feels threatened by a stupid caricature in a low-circulation Danish newspaper. The fundamentalist Islamic terror is *not* grounded in the terrorists' conviction of their superiority and in their desire to safeguard their cultural-religious identity from the onslaught of global consumerist civilisation. The problem with fundamentalists is not that we consider them inferior to us, but rather that *they themselves* secretly consider themselves inferior. This is why our condescending, politically correct assurances that we feel no superiority towards them only make them more furious and feeds their resentment. The problem is not cultural difference (their effort to preserve their identity), but the opposite fact that the fundamentalists are already like us, that secretly they have already internalised our standards and measure themselves by them. (This clearly goes for the Dalai Lama, who justifies Tibetan Buddhism in Western terms of the pursuit of happiness and the avoidance of pain.) Paradoxically, what the fundamentalists really lack is precisely a dose of that true "racist" conviction of one's own superiority.

The perplexing fact about the "terrorist" attacks is that they do not fit our standard opposition of evil as egotism or disregard for the common good, and good as the spirit of and actual readiness for sacrifice in the name of some higher cause. Terrorists cannot but appear as something akin to Milton's Satan with his "Evil, be thou my Good"[9]: while they pursue what appear to us to be evil goals with evil means, the very *form* of their activity meets the highest standard of the good. The resolution of this enigma isn't difficult and was already known to Rousseau. Egotism, or the concern for one's well-being, is *not* opposed to the common good, since altruistic norms can easily be deduced from egotist concerns.[10] Individualism versus communitarianism, utilitarianism versus the assertion of universal norms, are *false* oppositions since the two opposed options amount to the same in their result. The critics who complain how, in today's hedonistic-egotistic society, true values are lacking totally miss the point. The true opposite of egotist self-love is not altruism, a concern for common good, but envy, *ressentiment,* which makes me act *against* my own interests. Freud knew it well: the death drive is opposed to the pleasure principle as well as to the reality principle. The true evil, which is the death drive, involves self-sabotage. It makes us act *against* our own interests.[11]

The problem with human desire is that, as Lacan put it, it is always "desire of the Other" in all the senses of that term: desire for the Other, desire to be desired by the Other, and especially desire for what the Other desires.[12] This last makes envy, which includes resentment, constitutive components of human desire, something Augustine knew well. Recall the passage from his *Confessions,* often quoted by Lacan, the scene of a baby jealous of his brother suckling at the mother's breast: "I myself have seen and known an infant to be jealous though it could not speak. It became pale, and cast bitter looks on its foster-brother."

Based on this insight, Jean-Pierre Dupuy proposes a convincing critique of John Rawls's theory of justice.[13]

In the Rawlsian model of a just society, social inequalities are tolerated only insofar as they also help those at the bottom of the social ladder, and insofar as they are based not on inherited hierarchies, but on natural inequalities, which are considered contingent, not merits.[14] Even the British Conservatives seem now to be prepared to endorse Rawls's notion of justice: in December 2005 David Cameron, the newly elected Tory leader, signalled his intention of turning the Conservative Party into a defender of the underprivileged, declaring, "I think the test of all our policies should be: what does it do for the people who have the least, the people on the bottom rung of the ladder?" But what Rawls doesn't see is how such a society would create conditions for an uncontrolled explosion of *ressentiment*: in it, I would know that my lower status is fully "justified" and would thus be deprived of the ploy of excusing my failure as the result of social injustice.

Rawls thus proposes a terrifying model of a society in which hierarchy is directly legitimised in natural properties, thereby missing the simple lesson an anecdote about a Slovene peasant makes palpably clear. The peasant is given a choice by a good witch. She will either give him one cow and his neighbour two cows, or she'll take one cow from him and two from his neighbour. The peasant immediately chooses the second option.[15] Gore Vidal demonstrates the point succinctly: "It is not enough for me to win–the other must lose." The catch of envy/resentment is that it not only endorses the zero-sum game principle where my victory equals the other's loss. It also implies a gap between the two, which is not the positive gap (we can all win with no losers at all), but a negative one. If I have to choose between my gain and my opponent's loss, I prefer the opponent's loss, even if it means also a loss to me. It is as if my eventual gain from the opponent's loss functions as a kind of pathological element that stains the purity of my victory.

Friedrich Hayek knew that it was much easier to accept inequalities if one can claim that they result from an impersonal blind force: the good thing about the "irrationality" of the market and success or failure in capitalism is that it allows me precisely to perceive my failure or success as "undeserved," contingent.[16] Remember the old motif of the market as the modern version of an imponderable fate. The fact that capitalism is not "just" is thus a key feature of what makes it acceptable to the majority. I can live with my failure much more easily if I know that it is not due to my inferior qualities, but to chance.

What Nietzsche and Freud share is the idea that justice as equality is founded on envy–on the envy of the Other who has what we do not have, and who enjoys it. The demand for justice is thus ultimately the demand that the excessive enjoyment of the Other should be curtailed so that everyone's access to *jouissance* is equal. The necessary outcome of this demand, of course, is asceticism. Since it is not possible to impose equal *jouissance,* what is imposed instead to be equally shared is *prohibition.* Today, in our allegedly permissive society, however, this asceticism assumes the form of its opposite, a *generalised* superego injunction, the command "Enjoy!" We are all under the spell of this injunction.

The outcome is that our enjoyment is more hindered than ever. Take the yuppie who combines narcissistic "self-fulfilment" with those utterly ascetic disciplines of jogging, eating health food, and so on. Perhaps this is what Nietzsche had in mind with his notion of the Last Man, though it is only today that we can really discern his contours in the guise of the hedonistic asceticism of yuppies. Nietzsche wasn't simply urging life-assertion against asceticism: he was well aware that a certain asceticism is the obverse of a decadent excessive sensuality. His criticism of Wagner's *Parsifal,* and more generally of late-Romantic decadence which oscillates between damp sensuality and obscure spiritualism, makes the point.[17]

So what *is* envy? Let's return to the Augustinian scene of a sibling envying his brother who is suckling at the mother's breast. The subject does not envy the Other's possession of the prized object as such, but rather the way the Other is able to *enjoy* this object, which is why it is not enough for him simply to steal and thus gain possession of the object. His true aim is to destroy the Other's ability/capacity to enjoy the object. So we see that envy needs to be placed within the triad of envy, thrift, and melancholy, the three forms of not being able to enjoy the object and, of course, reflexively enjoying that very impossibility. In contrast to the subject of envy, who envies the other's possession and/or *jouissance* of the object, the miser possesses the object, but cannot enjoy/consume it. His satisfaction derives from just possessing it, elevating it into a sacred, untouchable/prohibited entity which should under no conditions be consumed. The proverbial figure of the lone miser is the one we see returning home, safely locking the doors, opening up his chest, and then taking that secret peek at his prized object, observing it in awe. The very thing that prevents his consumption of the object guarantees its status as the object of desire. As for the melancholic subject, like the miser he possesses the object, but he loses the reason that made him desire it. Most tragic of all, the melancholic has free access to all he wants, but finds no satisfaction in it.[18]

This excess of envy is the base of Rousseau's well-known, but none the less not fully exploited, distinction between egotism, *amour-de-soi* (that love of the self which is natural), and *amour-propre*, the perverted preferring of oneself to others in which a person focuses not on achieving a goal, but on destroying the obstacle to it:

> The primitive passions, which all directly tend towards our happiness, make us deal only with objects which relate to them, and whose principle is only amour-de-soi, are all in their essence lovable and tender; however, when, *diverted from their objects by obstacles, they are more occupied with the obstacle they try to get rid of, than with the object they try to reach,* they change their nature and become irascible and hateful. This is how amour-de-soi, which is a noble and absolute feeling, becomes amour-propre, that is to say, a relative feeling by means of which one compares oneself, a feeling which demands preferences, *whose enjoyment is purely negative and which does not strive to find satisfaction in our own well-being, but only in the misfortune of others.*[19]

An evil person is thus *not* an egotist, "thinking only about his own interests." A true egotist is too busy taking care of his own good to have time to cause misfortune to others. The primary vice of a bad person is precisely that he is more preoccupied with others than with himself. Rousseau is describing a precise libidinal mechanism: the inversion which generates the shift of the libidinal investment from the object to the obstacle itself. This could well be applied to fundamentalist violence–be it the Oklahoma bombings or the attack on the Twin Towers. In both cases, we were dealing with hatred pure and simple: destroying the obstacle, the Oklahoma City Federal Building, the World Trade Center, was what really mattered, not achieving the noble goal of a truly Christian or Muslim society.[20]

Here is why egalitarianism itself should never be accepted at its face value: the notion (and practice) of egalitarian justice, insofar as it is sustained by envy, relies on the inversion of the standard renunciation accomplished to benefit others: "I am ready to renounce it, *so that others will (also) NOT (be able to) have it!*" Far from being opposed to the spirit of sacrifice, evil here emerges as the very spirit of sacrifice, ready to ignore one's own well-being–if, through my sacrifice, I can deprive the Other of his *enjoyment . . .*

The Subject Supposed to Loot and Rape

One of the pop heroes of the U.S.–Iraq war, who enjoyed a brief run of celebrity fame, was Muhammad Saeed al-Sahaf, the unfortunate Iraqi information minister. In his daily press conferences, he heroically denied even the most evident facts and stuck to the Iraqi line.

When U.S. tanks were only hundreds of yards from his office, he continued to claim that the U.S. TV images of tanks on the Baghdad streets were just Hollywood special effects. Sometimes, however, he struck an oddly truthful chord: when confronted with the claims that Americans were in control of parts of Baghdad, he snapped back: "They are not in control of anything—they don't even control themselves!"

With the reports of New Orleans' descent into chaos, Marx's old saying that tragedy repeats itself as farce seems to have been inverted: Saeed's comic repartee turned into tragedy. The U.S., the world's policeman who endeavours to control threats to peace, freedom, and democracy around the globe, lost control of a part of America itself. For a few days, New Orleans apparently regressed to a wild preserve of looting, killing, and rape. It became a city of the dead and dying, a post-apocalyptic zone where those the philosopher Giorgio Agamben calls *Homini sacer*—people excluded from the civil order—wander. A fear permeates our lives that this kind of disintegration of the entire social fabric can come at any time, that some natural or techno-logical accident—whether earthquake or electricity failure or the hoary Millennium Bug—will reduce our world to a primitive wilderness. This sense of the fragility of our social bond is in itself a social symptom. Precisely when and where one would expect a surge of solidarity in the face of disaster, there is a fear that the most ruthless egotism will explode, in the way it did in New Orleans.

This is no time for any kind of *Schadenfreude* of "the U.S. got what it deserved" variety. The tragedy in New

Orleans was immense: analysis of what happened is overdue. The scenes we saw on the TV news in the last days cannot but recall a whole series of real-life media and cultural phenomena. The first association, of course, is that of the TV reports from Third World cities descending into chaos during a civil war (Kabul, Baghdad, Somalia, Liberia . . .)–and this accounts for the true surprise of the New Orleans eclipse: what we were used to seeing happening THERE was now taking place HERE. The irony is that Louisiana *is* often designated as the "U.S. banana republic," the Third World within the U.S. This is probably one of the reasons the reaction of the authorities came too late. Although rationally we knew what might happen, we didn't really believe that it would or could happen, just as with the threat of ecological catastrophe. We know all about it, but we somehow don't really believe that it can happen . . . [21]

So what *was* the catastrophe that took place in New Orleans? On closer inspection, the first thing to note is its strange temporality, a kind of delayed reaction. Immediately after the hurricane struck, there was momentary relief: its eye had missed New Orleans by about twenty-five miles. Only ten people were reported dead, so the worst, the feared catastrophe, had been avoided. Then, in the aftermath, things started to go badly wrong. Part of the protective levee of the city broke down. The city was flooded and social order disintegrated . . . The natural catastrophe, the hurricane, thus revealed itself to be "socially mediated" in multiple ways. First, there are good reasons to suspect that the U.S. is getting more hurricanes than usual owing to man-induced global warming. Second, the catastrophic immediate effect of the hurricane–the flooding of the city–was to a large extent due to human failure: the protective dams were not good enough, and the authorities were insufficiently prepared to meet the easily predictable humanitarian needs which followed. But the true and greater shock took place *after the event,* in the guise of the social effect of the natural catastrophe. The disintegration of the social order came as a kind of deferred action, as if natural catastrophe were repeating itself as social catastrophe.

How are we to read this social breakdown? The first reaction is the standard conservative one. The events in New Orleans confirm yet again how fragile social order is, how we need strict law enforcement and ethical pressure to prevent the explosion of violent passions. Human nature is naturally evil, descent into social chaos is a permanent threat . . . This argument can also be given a racist twist: those who exploded into violence were almost exclusively black, so here we have new proof of how blacks are not really civilised. Natural catastrophes bring to light the scum which is barely kept hidden and under check in normal times.

Of course, the obvious answer to this line of argument is that the New Orleans descent into chaos rendered visible the persisting racial divide in the U.S. New Orleans was 68 per cent black. The blacks are the poor and the underprivileged. They had no means by which to flee the city in time. They were left behind, starving and uncared for. No wonder they exploded. Their violent reaction should be seen as echoing the Rodney King riots in LA, or even the Detroit and Newark outbursts in the late 1960s.

More fundamentally, what if the tension that led to

the explosion in New Orleans was not the tension between "human nature" and the force of civilisation that
keeps it in check, but the tension between the two aspects of our civilisation itself? What if, in endeavouring
to control explosions like the one in New Orleans, the
forces of law and order were confronted with the very
nature of capitalism at its purest, the logic of individu-
alist competition, of ruthless self-assertion, generated
by capitalist dynamics, a "nature" much more threatening and violent than all the hurricanes and earth-
quakes?

In his theory of the sublime (*das Erhabene*), Immanuel Kant interpreted our fascination at the outbursts of
the power of nature as a negative proof of the superiority of spirit over nature. No matter how brutal the display of ferocious nature is, it cannot touch the moral
law in ourselves. Does the catastrophe of New Orleans
not provide a similar example of the sublime? No matter how brutal the vortex of the hurricane, it cannot
disrupt the vortex of the capitalist dynamic.

There is, however, another aspect of the New Orleans
outbursts that is no less crucial with regard to the ideological mechanisms that regulate our lives. According to
a well-known anthropological anecdote, the "primitives"
to whom one attributes certain superstitious beliefs–that
they descend from a fish or from a bird, for example–
when asked directly about these beliefs, answer: "Of
course not–we're not that stupid! But I was told that some
of our ancestors effectively did believe that . . ." In short,
they transfer their belief onto another. We do the same
with our children. We go through the ritual of Santa
Claus, since our children are *supposed* to believe in him

and we do not want to disappoint them. They pretend to believe so as not to disappoint us and our belief in their naivety (and to get the presents, of course). Is this not also the usual excuse of the mythical crooked politician who turns honest?–"I cannot disappoint the ordinary people who believe in it (or in me)." To take this a step further, is this need to find another who "really believes" not the very thing which propels us in our need to stigmatise the Other as a (religious or ethnic) "fundamentalist"? In an uncanny way, some beliefs always seem to function "at a distance": in order for the belief to function, there *has to be* some ultimate guarantor of it, yet this guarantor is always deferred, displaced, never present *in persona*. The point, of course, is that this other subject who fully believes need not exist for the belief to be operative. It is enough to *presuppose* his existence, that is, to *believe* in it, either in the guise of the primitive Other or in the guise of the impersonal "one" ("one believes . . .").

Doesn't this deferral or displacement also work for our innermost feelings and attitudes, including crying and laughing? From the so-called "weepers," women hired to cry at funerals in "primitive" societies, to the "canned laughter" of television sitcoms where the reaction of laughter to a comic scene is dubbed into the soundtrack, to the adoption of an avatar in cyberspace, the same sort of phenomenon is at work. When I construct a "false" image of myself which stands for me in a virtual community in which I participate (in sexual games, for example, a shy man often assumes the on-screen persona of an attractive promiscuous woman), the emotions I feel and "feign" as part of my onscreen persona are not simply false. Although what I experience as my "true self" does not feel them, they are none the less in a sense "true," just as when I watch a TV series replete with canned laughter, even if I do not laugh, but simply stare at the screen, tired after a hard day's work, I none the less feel relieved after the show . . . [22]

The events in New Orleans after the city was struck by hurricane Katrina provide a new addition to this series of "subjects supposed to . . .": *the subject supposed to loot and rape*. We all remember the reports on the disintegration of public order, the explosion of black violence, rape, and looting–however, later inquiries demonstrated that in the large majority of cases, these alleged orgies of violence simply *did not occur*: unverified rumours were reported as facts by the media. For example, on 4 September Superintendent Compass of the New Orleans Police Department was quoted in the *New York Times* about conditions at the convention centre: "The tourists are walking around there, and as soon as these individuals see them, they're being preyed upon. They are beating, they are raping them in the streets." In an interview two weeks later, he conceded that some of his most shocking statements turned out to be untrue: "We have no official reports to document any murder. Not one official report of rape or sexual assault."[23]

The reality of poor blacks abandoned and left without the means of survival was thus transformed into the spectre of an explosion of black violence, of tourists robbed and killed on streets that had slid into anarchy, in a Superdome rife with gangs raping women and children . . . These reports were not merely words, they were words which had precise *material effects*: they generated fears that led the authorities to change troop deployments, they delayed medical evacuations, drove police officers to quit, grounded helicopters. For example, Acadian Ambulance Company's cars were locked down after word came that a firehouse in Covington had been looted by armed robbers of all its water–a report that proved to be completely unfounded.

Of course, the sense of menace had been ignited by genuine disorder and violence: looting *did* begin at the moment the storm passed over New Orleans. It ranged from base thievery to foraging for the necessities of life. However, the (limited) reality of crimes in no way condones "reports" on the total breakdown of law and order, not because these reports were "exaggerated," but for a much more radical reason. Jacques Lacan claimed that, even if the patient's wife really is sleeping around with other men, the patient's jealousy is still to be treated as a pathological condition. In a homologous way, even if rich Jews in the Germany of the early 1930s "really" exploited German workers, seduced their daughters, dominated the popular press, and so on, Nazi anti-Semitism was still emphatically "untrue," a pathological ideological condition. Why? What made it pathological was the disavowed libidinal investment into the figure of the Jew. The cause of all social antagonisms was projected into the "Jew," the object of a perverted love-hatred, the spectral figure of mixed fascination and disgust. Exactly the same applies to the looting in New Orleans: *even if ALL reports of violence and rape were to be proved factually true, the stories circulating about them would still be "pathological" and racist,* since what motivated these stories was not facts, but racist prejudices, the satisfaction felt by those who would be able to say: "You see, blacks are really like that, violent barbarians under the thin layer of civilisation!" In other words, we would be dealing with what one can call *lying in the guise of truth:* even if what I am saying is factually true, the motives that make me say it are false.

So what about the obvious rightist-populist counter-argument: if telling factual truth involves a subjective lie–the racist attitude–does this mean that, out of political correctness, we are not allowed to tell the simple facts when blacks commit a crime? The answer is clear: the obligation is not to lie, to falsify or ignore facts, on behalf of some higher political truth, but–and this is a much more difficult thing to do–to change one's subjective position so that telling the factual truth will not involve the lie of the subjective position of enunciation. Therein resides the limitation of standard political correctness: instead of changing the subjective position from which we speak, it imposes on us a set of rules with regard to content. Don't point out that blacks committed crimes. Don't mention how lesbian couples mistreat their children. Don't dwell on how underprivileged minorities brutalise women and children . . . But all these rules on content effectively leave our subjective position untouched.

Of course, we do not openly admit these motives. From time to time they nevertheless pop up in our public space in censored form, in the guise of de-negation, evoked as an option and then immediately discarded. Recall what William Bennett, the gambling, neo-con author of *The Book of Virtues,* said on 28 September

2005 on his call-in programme *Morning in America*: "But I do know that it's true that if you wanted to reduce crime, you could, if that were your sole purpose, you could abort every black baby in this country, and your crime rate would go down. That would be an impossibly ridiculous and morally reprehensible thing to do, but your crime rate would go down." The White House reacted immediately: "The president believes the comments were not appropriate." Two days later, Bennett qualified his statement: "I was putting a hypothetical proposition . . . and then said about it, it was morally reprehensible to recommend abortion of an entire group of people. But this is what happens when you argue that ends can justify the means." This is exactly what Freud meant when he wrote that the unconscious knows no negation: the official (Christian, democratic . . .) discourse is accompanied and sustained by a whole nest of obscene, brutal, racist, sexist fantasies, which can only be admitted in a censored form.

But we are not dealing here only with good old racism. Something more is at stake: a fundamental feature of our emerging "global" society. On 11 September 2001 the Twin Towers were hit. Twelve years earlier, on 9 November 1989, the Berlin Wall fell. That date heralded the "happy '90s," the Francis Fukuyama dream of the "end of history"–the belief that liberal democracy had, in principle, won; that the search was over; that the advent of a global, liberal world community lurked just around the corner; that the obstacles to this ultra-Hollywood happy ending were merely empirical and contingent (local pockets of resistance where the leaders did not yet grasp that their time was up). In contrast, 9/11 is the main symbol of the end of the Clintonite happy '90s. This is the era in which new walls emerge everywhere, between Israel and the West Bank, around the European Union, on the U.S.–Mexico border. The rise of the populist New Right is just the most prominent example of the urge to raise new walls.

A couple of years ago, an ominous decision of the European Union passed almost unnoticed: the plan to establish an all-European border police force to secure the isolation of Union territory and thus to prevent the influx of immigrants. *This* is the truth of globalisation: the construction of new walls safeguarding prosperous Europe from the immigrant flood. One is tempted to resuscitate here the old Marxist "humanist" opposition of "relations between things" and "relations between persons": in the much-celebrated free circulation opened up by global capitalism, it is "things" (commodities) which freely circulate, while the circulation of "persons" is more and more controlled. We are not dealing now with "globalisation" as an unfinished project but with a true "dialectics of globalisation": the segregation of the people *is* the reality of economic globalisation. This new racism of the developed is in a way much more brutal than the previous ones: its implicit legitimisation is neither naturalist (the "natural" superiority of the developed West) nor any longer culturalist (we in the West also want to preserve our cultural identity), but unabashed economic egotism. The fundamental divide is one between those included in the sphere of (relative) economic prosperity and those excluded from it.

This brings us back to rumours and so-called reports about "subjects supposed to loot and rape." New Orleans is among the cities most heavily marked by the internal wall within the U.S. that separates the affluent from the ghettoised blacks. And it is about those on the other side of the wall that we fantasise: more and more they live in another world, in a blank zone that offers itself as a screen for the projection of our fears, anxieties, and secret desires. *The "subject supposed to loot and rape" is on the other side of the wall.* It is about this subject that Bennett can afford to make his slip of the tongue and confess in a censored mode his murderous dreams. More than anything else, rumours and false reports from the aftermath of Katrina bear witness to the deep class division of American society.

When, at the beginning of October 2005, the Spanish police dealt with the problem of how to stop the influx of desperate African immigrants who tried to penetrate the small Spanish territory of Melilla, on the Rif coast of Africa, they displayed plans to build a wall between the Spanish enclave and Morocco. The images presented–a complex structure replete with electronic equipment–bore an uncanny resemblance to the Berlin Wall, only with the opposite function. This wall was destined to prevent people from coming in, not getting out. The cruel irony of the situation is that it is the government of José Zapatero, at this moment leader of arguably the most anti-racist and tolerant administration in Europe, that is forced to adopt these measures of segregation. This is a clear sign of the limit of the multiculturalist "tolerant" approach, which preaches open borders and acceptance of others. If one were to open the borders, the first to rebel would be the local working classes. It is thus becoming clear that the solution is not

"tear down the walls and let them all in," the easy empty
demand of soft-hearted liberal "radicals." The only true
solution is to tear down the *true* wall, not the Immigra-
tion Department one, but the socio-economic one: to
change society so that people will no longer desperately
try to escape their own world.

Presto

ANTINOMIES OF TOLERANT REASON

Liberalism or Fundamentalism?
A Plague on Both Their Houses!

Immanuel Kant developed the notion of the "antinomies of pure reason." Finite human reason inevitably falls into self-contradiction when it attempts to go beyond concrete sense experience to address such questions as: Does the Universe have a beginning in time, a limit in space, an initial cause, or is it infinite? The antinomy arises because it is possible to construct valid arguments for both sides of the question: we can conclusively demonstrate that the universe is finite *and* that it is infinite. Kant argues that if this conflict of reason is not resolved, humanity will lapse into a bleak scepticism which he called the "euthanasia of pure reason."[1] The reactions to the Muslim outrage at the Danish caricatures of Muhammad–the other violent outburst that stirred public opinion in the West in the autumn of 2005–seem to confront us with a similar antinomy of *tolerant* reason: two opposite stories can be told about the caricatures, each of them convincing and well argued, without any possibility of mediation or reconciliation between them.

To the Western liberal for whom freedom of the press is one of the highest goods, the case is clear. Even if we reject the caricatures in disgust, their publication in no way justifies murderous mob viovlence and the stigmatisation of a whole country. Those offended by the caricatures should have gone to court to prosecute the offender, and not demanded apologies from a state which espouses press freedom. The Muslim reaction displays a blatant lack of understanding of the Western principle of an independent civil society.

What underlies the Muslim attitude is the Muslim belief in the sacred status of writing (which is why, traditionally, Muslims don't use paper in their toilets). The idea of thoroughly secularised writing, not to mention a Monty Pythonesque "Life of Muhammad," is unimaginable in an Islamic culture. There is more in this than may at first appear. A mocking of divinity is part of European religious tradition itself, starting with the ancient Greek ritualistic ridiculing of the gods of Olympus. There is nothing subversive or atheist here: this mocking is an inherent part of religious life. As for Christianity, we must not forget the moments of carnivalesque irony in Christ's parables and riddles. Even the crucifixion contains its own mocking, blasphemous spectacle in the donkey-riding king who is Christ, his crown a matter of thorns. Christianity disrupts the pagan notion of the slapstick reversal of the proper relations of authority in which, for a limited time, a fool is celebrated as a king. In Christianity, the "true" king is revealed to be his own blasphemy, a Lord of Misrule, a fool. This is why when, in December 2006, a group of Polish conservative-nationalist members of parliament seriously proposed to proclaim Jesus Christ king of Poland, they not only confused religious and political orders; their proposal was also deeply *pagan,* anti-Christian, missing as it did the joke of Christianity itself.

For the Western liberal there is also the problem of the brutal and vulgar anti-Semitic and anti-Christian caricatures that abound in the press and schoolbooks of Muslim countries. There is no respect here for other people and their religion–a respect that is demanded from the West. But there is little respect for their own people, either, as the case of a particular cleric exemplifies. In the autumn of 2006, Sheik Taj Din al-Hilali, Australia's most senior Muslim cleric, caused a furore when, after a group of Muslim men had been jailed for gang rape, he said: "If you take uncovered meat and place it outside on the street . . . and the cats come and eat it . . . whose fault is it–the cats' or the uncovered meat? The uncovered meat is the problem." The explosively provocative nature of this comparison between a woman who is not veiled and raw, uncovered meat distracted attention from another, much more surprising premise underlying al-Hilali's argument: if women are held responsible for the sexual conduct of men, does this not imply that men are totally helpless when faced with what they perceive as sexual temptation, that they are simply unable to resist it, that they are utterly in thrall to their sexual hunger, precisely like a cat when it sees raw meat?[2] In contrast to this presumption of a complete lack of male responsibility for their own sexual conduct, the emphasis on public female eroticism in the West relies on the premise that men *are* capable of sexual restraint, that they are not blind slaves of their sexual drives.[3]

Some of the Western partisans of multiculturalist tolerance, who try to display "understanding" of the Muslim reaction, point out that the obvious overreaction to the caricatures has an underlying cause. The murderous violence at first aimed at Denmark, but then expanding to the whole of Europe and the West, indicates that the protests were not really about the specific cartoons, but about the humiliations and frustrations associated with the West's entire imperialist attitude. In the weeks after the demonstrations, journalists competed with each other to enumerate the "real reasons" behind the riots: the Israeli occupation, dissatisfaction with the pro-American Musharraf regime in Pakistan, anti-Americanism in Iran, and so on. The problem with this line of excuse is clear if we extend it to anti-Semitism itself: Muslim anti-Semitism is not "really" about Jews, but a displaced protest about capitalist exploitation. But this excuse only makes it worse for the Muslims and forces one logically to ask: why don't they address the TRUE cause?

On the other hand, a no less convincing case can be made against the West. It soon became known that the same Danish newspaper that published the Muhammad caricatures, in a blatant display of bias, had previously rejected caricatures of Christ as too offensive. Furthermore, prior to resorting to public manifestations, the Danish Muslims did for months try the "European" path of dialogue, asking to be seen by government authorities. They were ignored. The reality behind all this is the sad fact of the rising xenophobia in Denmark, signalling the end of the myth of Scandinavian tolerance. Finally, we should examine the various prohibitions and limitations which underlie the so-called freedom of the press in the West. Isn't the

Holocaust a sacred and untouchable fact? At the very moment when the Muslim protests were raging, the British historian David Irving was in an Austrian prison serving a three-year term for expressing his doubts about the Holocaust in an article published fifteen years earlier.[4]

How are we to read such legal prohibitions against (publicly) doubting the fact(s) of the Holocaust? The common moral sense which tells us that there is something false here is correct: the legalisation of the untouchable status of the Holocaust is, in a sense, the most refined and perverted version of Holocaust denial.[5] While fully admitting the fact(s) of the Holocaust, such laws neutralise their symbolic efficiency. Through their existence, the memory of the Holocaust is externalised, so the individual is exempted from its impact. I can calmly reply to the critics: "It is written in our law and dealt with. So the problem is taken care of. What more do you want? Leave me to lead my life in peace now!" The idea, of course, is not that we occasionally need a David Irving to resuscitate our historical memory of the Holocaust and awaken us from the dogmatic slumber of relying on official external (ised) memory. It is that sometimes, a direct admission of a crime can be the most efficient way to avoid responsibility for it.

The Muslim counterpart to this legalistic hypocrisy is the strange inconsistency in their own references to the Holocaust. The Jordanian newspaper *Ad-Dustour* on 19 October 2003 published a cartoon depicting the railway to the death camp at Auschwitz-Birkenau, with Israeli flags replacing the Nazi ones. The sign in

Arabic reads: "Gaza Strip or the Israeli Annihilation
Camp." (It is interesting to note how this identification
of the Israeli army with the Nazis was strangely echoed
by the settlers in Gaza who, when they were forcibly
evacuated by the IDF, also identified the buses and
trucks provided by the IDF with the trains that took
the Jews to Auschwitz, and claimed that another Holocaust, another destruction of the Jewish nation,
would come to pass if these new transports were not
stopped. Two opposite and mirroring examples of the
brutal instrumentalisation of the Holocaust meet
here.) This idea that Israel's policies towards the Palestinians have been comparable to Nazi actions towards
Jews strangely contradicts Holocaust denial. The joke
evoked by Freud in order to render the strange logic
of dreams gives us a useful gloss on the strange logic
at work here: (1) I never borrowed a kettle from you;
(2) I returned it to you unbroken; (3) the kettle was
already broken when I got it from you. Such an enu-
meration of inconsistent arguments, of course, confirms by negation what it endeavours to deny–that I
returned your kettle broken . . . Doesn't this very inconsistency characterise the way radical Islamists respond to the Holocaust? (1) The Holocaust did not
happen; (2) it did happen, but the Jews deserved it; (3)
the Jews did not deserve it, but they have lost the right
to complain by doing to Palestinians what the Nazis
did to them.

Speaking in Mecca in December 2005, President
Ahmadinejad of Iran implied that guilt for the Holocaust led European countries to support the establishment of the state of Israel:

Some European countries insist on saying that Hitler killed millions of innocent Jews in furnaces, and they insist on it to the extent that if anyone proves something contrary to that, they condemn that person and throw them in jail . . . Although we don't accept this claim, if we suppose it is true, our question for the Europeans is: Is the killing of innocent Jewish people by Hitler the reason for their support of the occupiers of Jerusalem? . . . If the Europeans are honest, they should give some of their provinces in Europe—in Germany, Austria, or other countries—to the Zionists, and the Zionists can establish their state in Europe. You offer part of Europe, and we will support it.[6]

This statement is both disgusting and contains an insight. The disgusting part is, of course, Holocaust denial and, even more problematically, the claim that the Jews deserved the Holocaust. ("We don't accept this claim": which one? That Hitler killed million of Jews *or that the Jews were innocent* and did not deserve to be killed?) What is correct about the quoted statement is the reminder of European hypocrisy: the European manoeuvre was indeed to pay for its own guilt with another people's land. So when the Israeli government spokesman Ra'anan Gissin said in response, "Just to remind Mr. Ahmadinejad, we've been here long before his ancestors were here. Therefore, we have a birthright to be here in the land of our forefathers and to live here," he evoked a historical right which, when applied universally, would lead to universal slaughter. That is to say, can one imagine a world in which ethnic groups would continually "remind" their neighbours that "we've been here before you"–even if this means a thousand or more years ago–and use this fact to justify their effort to seize the neighbour's land? Along these lines, a French Jewish writer, Cecile Winter, proposed a nice mental experiment: imagine Israel as it is, and its trajectory over the last half-century, *ignoring* the fact that Jews came there stigmatised by the signifier of the absolute victim, and thus beyond moral reproach. What we get, in that case, is a standard story of colonisation.[7]

But why should we *abstract* from the Holocaust when we judge Israeli politics towards Palestinians? Not because one can compare the two, but precisely because the Holocaust *was* an incomparably graver crime. The very need to evoke the Holocaust in defence of Israeli acts secretly implies that Israel is committing such horrible crimes that only the absolute trump card of the Holocaust can redeem them. Does this then mean that one should ignore the fact of the Holocaust when dealing with actual politics, since every use of it to legitimise political acts amounts to its obscene instrumentalisation? This, none the less, comes all too close to the (pseudo-)leftist obscenity according to which any mention of the Holocaust in today's political discourse is a fake, a manipulation to obfuscate Israeli crimes against the Palestinians (or, more generally, to minimise the no-less-terrifying suffering of Third World people, with regard to which the reference to the Holocaust enables the colonisers to present themselves as the true and ultimate victims). We are thus caught in a Kantian antinomy (though it would be too obscene to call this "the antinomy of Holocaust reason"): while any positive reference to the Holocaust amounts to its instrumentalisation, the reduction of any reference to the Holocaust to such an instrumentalisation (i.e., the imposition of total silence about the Holocaust in political discourse) is no less unacceptable.

But perhaps this reference to Kant also provides a solution: along the lines of Kant's notion of the negative use of reason as the only legitimate one when we are dealing with noumenal objects, one should limit its use to a negative mode. The only permitted reference to the Holocaust should be a negative one. The Holocaust should not be evoked to justify/legitimise any political measures, but only to delegitimise (some) such measures, to impose some limitations on our political acts: one is justified in condemning acts which display a hubris whose extreme expression was the Holocaust.

What, then, if the true caricatures of Islam are the violent anti-Danish demonstrations themselves, offering up a ridiculous image of Islam which exactly fits the Western cliché? The ultimate irony, of course, is that the ire of Muslim crowds turned against that very Europe which staunch anti-Islamists, such as the notorious journalist Oriana Fallaci who died in September 2006, perceived as far too tolerant towards Islam, and already capitulating to its pressure; and within Europe, against Denmark, part of the very model of tolerance Scandinavia stands for. This constellation perfectly reproduces the paradox of the superego: the more you obey what the Other demands of you, the guiltier you are. It is as if the more you tolerate Islam, the stronger its pressure on you will be.

Oriana Fallaci was the intolerant woman who served as a symptom of tolerant men. In the books written in her last years, she broke two cardinal rules: her writing was passionate and fully engaged; she utterly disregarded the politically correct mantra of respect for the Other.[8] Her claim was that the ongoing War on Terror was not a clash of civilisations, but a clash between civilisation and barbarism. The enemy is not the political misuse of Islam, but Islam itself. The danger from within is the compromising attitude predominant in Europe. Her thesis is that Europe has already spiritually capitulated: it treats itself as a province of Islam, afraid of asserting its cultural and political identity. Repeatedly Fallaci draws attention to the asymmetry of tolerance: Europe apologises all the time, supports the construction of new mosques, urges respect, and so on. Meanwhile in some Muslim countries, the very conversion from Islam to Christianity is punishable by death. Fallaci's adamant stance is perhaps why her books are marginalised and perceived as unacceptable: after every big call to rally against the fundamentalist threat, Bush, Blair, and even Sharon never forget to praise Islam as a great religion of love and tolerance which has nothing to do with the disgusting terrorist acts carried out in its name.

Fallaci was an enlightened liberal atheist, not a Christian fundamentalist, and it is all too easy to dismiss her last books as an outburst of hysterical racist reaction. Her extraordinary success turned her into something of an "untouchable" excremental object: the very embarrassment she provoked in multiculturalist liberals demonstrated that she had touched liberalism's sore point, its very own "repressed."

But Fallaci's mistake was to take the multiculturalist

subservient "respect" for the Muslim Other seriously. She failed to see how this "respect" is a fake, a sign of hidden and patronising racism. In other words, far from simply opposing multiculturalist tolerance, what Fallaci did was to bring out its disavowed core. The French philosopher Alain Finkielkraut said in an interview published on 18 November 2005 in *Ha'aretz*, commenting on the French suburban outbursts: "If an Arab burns a school, it is a revolt. If a white man does it, it is fascism . . . Step by step, the generous idea of a war on racism is monstrously turning into a lying ideology. Anti-racism will be to the twenty-first century what communism was to the twentieth century. A source of violence." Finkielkraut is right here, but for the wrong reasons: what is wrong in the politically correct multiculturalist struggle against racism is not its excessive anti-racism, but its covert racism.

Let us compare two statements by George W. Bush to look at this. In his inauguration speech in February 2005, Bush proclaimed: "America will not pretend that jailed dissidents prefer their chains or that women welcome humiliation and servitude." Alongside this we need to place Bush's repeated claims that Islam is a great religion of peace and is only *misused* by fundamentalists. A liberal multiculturalist would tend to dismiss the first claim as an expression of cultural imperialism, and qualify the second as acceptable, though really a mask for hypocrisy. Perhaps one should turn this assessment round and fearlessly follow it to its conclusion. What is problematic about Bush's "respect for Islam" claims is not their hypocrisy, but the fact that they cover up an underlying racism and Eurocentrist cultural imperialism.

What is wrong is the very content of his claims. The game of redeeming the inner truth of a religion or ideology and separating this out from its later or secondary political exploitation is simply false. It is non-philosophical. One needs to be ruthless here, with regard to Islam, Christianity . . . or indeed Marxism. What is hypocritical is in fact Bush's first statement: one should fully endorse its content, noting at the same time that Bush's political acts do not follow suit.

The Jerusalem Chalk Circle

It is, however, all too easy to score points in this debate using witty reversals which can go on indefinitely; so let us stop this imagined polemical dialogue and risk a direct step into the "heart of darkness" of the Middle East conflict. Many conservative (and not only conservative) political thinkers, from Blaise Pascal to Immanuel Kant and Joseph de Maistre, elaborated the notion of the illegitimate origins of power, of the "founding crime" on which states are based, which is why one should offer "noble lies" to people in the guise of heroic narratives of origin. With regard to such ideas, what was often said about Israel is quite true: the misfortune of Israel is that it was established as a nation-state a century or two too late, in conditions when such founding crimes are no longer acceptable. The ultimate irony here is that it was Jewish intellectual influence that contributed to the rise of this unacceptability!

During my last visit to Israel, I was approached by an Israeli intellectual who, aware of my Palestinian sympathies, mockingly asked me: "Aren't you ashamed to be here, in Israel, in this illegal, criminal state? Aren't you afraid that your being here will contaminate your leftist credentials and make you an accomplice in crime?"

In all honesty I have to admit that every time I travel to Israel, I experience that strange thrill of entering a forbidden territory of illegitimate violence. Does this mean I am (not so) secretly an anti-Semite? But what if what disturbs me is precisely that I find myself in a state which hasn't yet obliterated the "founding violence" of its "illegitimate" origins, repressed them into a timeless past. In this sense, what the state of Israel confronts us with is merely the obliterated past of *every* state power.

Why are we more sensitive to this violence today? Precisely because, in a global universe which legitimises itself with a global morality, sovereign states are no longer exempt from moral judgments, but treated as moral agents to be punished for their crimes, however contested it might remain who exerts the justice and who judges the judge. State sovereignty is thus severely constrained. This accounts for the emblematic value of the Middle East conflict: it confronts us with the fragility and penetrability of the border that separates "illegitimate" non-state power from "legitimate" state power. In the case of the state of Israel, its "illegitimate" origins are not yet obliterated. Their effects are fully felt today. Bertolt Brecht's motto from his *Beggar's Opera* comes to mind: what is the robbery of a bank compared to the founding of a bank? In other words, what is the robbery that violates the law compared to the robbery that takes place within the confines of the law? One is tempted to propose a new variation of this motto: what is committing an act of terror to a state power waging war on terror?

When despairing Western observers wonder why the Palestinians persist in their stubborn attachment to their land and refuse to dissolve their identity in the wider Arab sea, they're demanding that Palestinians ignore precisely what is Israel's "illegitimate" state-founding violence. In a display of poetic justice that asserts the irony of history, the Palestinians are giving Israel back its own message in its inverted and true form. There is the pathological attachment to the land, implying the right to return to it thousands of years later—a de facto denial of the deterritorialisation that allegedly characterises today's global capitalism. But the inverted message goes further than that. Imagine if we were to read the following statement in today's media:

> Our enemies called us terrorists . . . People who were neither our friends nor our enemies . . . also used this Latin name . . . And yet, we were not terrorists . . . The historical and linguistic origins of the political term "terror" prove that it cannot be applied to a revolutionary war of liberation . . . Fighters for freedom must arm; otherwise they would be crushed overnight . . . What has a struggle for the dignity of man, against oppression and subjugation, to do with "terrorism"?

One would automatically attribute this to an Islamic terrorist group and condemn it. However, the author of these words is none other than Menachem Begin in the years when the Haganah was fighting the British forces in Palestine.[9] It is interesting to note how, in those years of the Jewish struggle against the British military in Palestine, the very term "terrorist" had a positive connotation. Here's another mental experiment: imagine reading in contemporary newspapers an open letter headed "Letter to the Terrorists of Palestine," containing these sentences:

> My Brave Friends. You may not believe what I write you, for there is a lot of fertilizer in the air at the moment. But on my word as an old reporter, what I write is true. The Palestinians of America are for you. You are their champions. You are the grin they wear. You are the feather in their hats. You are the first answer that makes sense–to the New World. Every time you blow up an Israeli arsenal, or wreck an Israeli jail, or send an Israeli railroad sky high, or rob an Israeli bank, or let go with your guns and bombs at the Israeli betrayers and invaders of your homeland, the Palestinians of America make a little holiday in their hearts.

A very similar open letter was indeed published in the late 1940s in American newspapers. It was written by none other than Ben Hecht, the celebrated Hollywood scriptwriter. All I have done is to replace the word "Jews" with "Palestinians" and "British" with "Israeli."[10] It is almost attractive to see the first-generation Israeli leaders openly confessing the fact that their claims to the land of Palestine cannot be grounded in universal justice, that we are dealing with a simple war of conquest between two groups between whom no mediation is possible. Here is what David Ben-Gurion, Israel's first prime minister, wrote:

> Everyone can see the weight of the problems in the relations between Arabs and Jews. But no one sees that

there is no solution to these problems. There is no
solution! Here is an abyss, and nothing can link its two
sides . . . We as a people want this land to be ours; the
Arabs as a people want this land to be theirs.[11]

The problem with this statement today is clear: such an
exemption of ethnic conflicts for land from moral considerations is simply no longer acceptable. This is why
the way the famous Nazi hunter Simon Wiesenthal, in
his *Justice Not Vengeance,* approaches this problem appears so deeply problematic:

Some day it will have to be realized that it is impossible
to establish a state without some people, who have been
living in the region, finding their rights curtailed.
(Because where no people have lived before it is
presumably impossible for people to live.) One has to be
content if these infringements are kept within bounds
and if relatively few people are affected by them. That
was the case when Israel was founded . . . After all, there
had been a Jewish population there for a long time, and
the Palestinian population was comparatively sparse
and had relatively numerous options in giving way.[12]

What Wiesenthal is advocating here is nothing less than
state-founding violence with a human face; a violence,
that is, with limited violations. (As for the comparative
sparsity of settlers, the population of the Palestinian
territory in 1880 was 25,000 Jews and 620,000 Palestinians.) However, from our present perspective, the most
interesting sentence in Wiesenthal's essay comes a
page earlier, where he writes: "The continually victorious state of Israel cannot forever rely on the sympathy

shown to victims."[13] Wiesenthal seems to mean that now that the state of Israel is "continually victorious," it no longer needs to behave like a victim, but can fully assert its force. This may be true, as long as one adds that this position of power also involves new responsibilities. The problem at the moment is that the state of Israel, though "continually victorious," still relies on the image of Jews as victims to legitimise its power politics, as well as to denounce its critics as covert Holocaust sympathisers. Arthur Koestler, the great anti-communist convert, proposed a profound insight: "If power corrupts, the reverse is also true; persecution corrupts the victims, though perhaps in subtler and more tragic ways."

This is the fatal flaw in the one strong argument for the creation of a Jewish nation-state after the Holocaust: in creating their own state, the Jews would overcome the situation of being delivered up to the mercy of the diaspora states and the tolerance or intolerance of their nation's majority. Although this line of argument is different from the religious one, it has to rely on religious tradition to justify the geographical location of this new state. Otherwise, one finds oneself in the situation of the old joke about a madman looking for his lost wallet under the street light and not in the dark corner where he has lost it, because one sees better under the light: because it was easier, the Jews took land from the Palestinians and not from those who caused them so much suffering and thus owed them reparation.

Robert Fisk, a British journalist who lives in Lebanon, made a documentary about the Middle East crisis in which he reports how his

Arab neighbours, Palestinian refugees, had shown him the key of the house that they had once owned in Haifa, before it was taken from them by Israelis. So he visited the Jewish family living in the house and asked them where *they* had come from. The answer was Chrzanow, a small town near Krakow, in Poland, and they showed him a photo of their former Polish home, which they had lost during the war. So he travelled to Poland, and sought out the woman living in the house in Chrzanow. She was a "repatriant" from Lemberg, now in Western Ukraine. It wasn't hard to guess the next link in the chain. The repatriate had been driven out of her home city when it was seized by the USSR. No doubt her house was taken over by Russians who had been brought in by the postwar regime in its campaign to Sovietize the city.[14]

And the story goes on, of course: this Russian family probably moved there from a home in Eastern Ukraine destroyed by the Germans in the heavy fighting on the Eastern Front . . . It is here that the Holocaust comes in: the reference to the Holocaust enables the Israelis to exempt themselves from this chain of substitutions. But those who evoke the Holocaust in this way effectively manipulate it, instrumentalising it for current political uses.

The big mystery of the Israeli–Palestinian conflict is why it has persisted for so long when everybody knows the only viable solution: the withdrawal of the Israelis from the West Bank and Gaza, the establishment of a Palestinian state, as well as some kind of a compromise concerning Jerusalem. Whenever agreement has seemed at hand, it has inexplicably disappeared. How often has it happened that just when peace seems a simple matter of finding a proper formulation for some minor statements, everything suddenly falls apart, displaying the frailty of the negotiated compromise? The Middle East conflict has taken on the cast of a neurotic symptom – everyone sees the way to get rid of the obstacle, and yet no one wants to remove it, as if there is some kind of pathological libidinal profit gained by persisting in the deadlock.

This is why the Middle East crisis is such a sensitive point for pragmatic politics, which aim at resolving problems step by step in a realistic way. In this case, what is utopian is the very notion that such a "realistic" approach will work, while the only "realistic" solution here is the *big* one, to solve the problem at its roots. The old motto from 1968 applies: *Soyons réalistes, demandons l'impossible!* Only a radical gesture that appears "impossible" within the existing coordinates will realistically do the job. Perhaps the solution "everybody knows" as the only viable one – the withdrawal of the Israelis from the West Bank and Gaza, the establishment of a Palestinian state – will not do, and one has to change the entire frame, shift the picture with the one-state solution at the horizon.

One is tempted to speak here of a symptomal *knot*: is it not that in the Israeli–Palestinian conflict the standard roles are somehow inverted, twisted around as in a knot? Israel – officially representing Western liberal modernity in the area – legitimises itself in terms of its ethnic-religious identity, while the Palestinians – decried as premodern "fundamentalists" – legitimise their demands in the terms of secular citizenship. (One is tempted to risk the hypothesis that it is the very Israeli occupation of the Palestinian territories which pushed Palestinians into perceiving themselves as a separate nation in search of their own state, not just as a part of the Arab mass.) We have the paradox of the state of Israel, the island of alleged liberal democratic modernity in the Middle East, countering the Arab demands with an even more "fundamentalist" ethnic-religious claim to their sacred land. The further irony is that according to some polls, Israelis are the most atheistic nation in the world: around 70 per cent of them do not believe in any kind of divinity. Their reference to the land thus relies on a fetishist disavowal: "I know very well that God doesn't exist, but I none the less believe that he gave us the land of Greater Israel . . ." And as the story of the Gordian knot tells us, the only way to resolve such a deadlock is not to unravel the knot, but to cut it. But how? Badiou recently addressed this impasse:

> The founding of a Zionist State was a mixed, thoroughly complex, reality. On the one side, it was an event which was part of a larger event: the rise of great revolutionary, communist and socialist projects, the idea of founding an entirely new society. On the other hand, it was a counter-event, part of a larger counter-event: colonialism, the brutal conquest by people who came from Europe of the new land where other people lived. Israel is an extraordinary mixture of revolution and reaction, of emancipation and oppression. The Zionist State needs to become what it had in itself of being just

and new. It has to become the least racial, the least religious, and the least nationalist of States. The most universal of them all.[15]

While there is a truth in this insight, the problem remains: can one really untie the knot in this direct way and simply separate the two aspects of Israel, in the sense of fulfilling the possibility of the revolutionary project of the Zionist state without its colonialising shadow? This is like the legendary "If . . ." answer of an American politician in the 1920s to the question "Do you support the prohibition of wine or not?": "If by wine you mean the terrible drink which ruined thousands of families, making husbands a wreck who were beating their wives and neglecting their children, then I am fully for the prohibition. But if you mean by wine the noble drink with a wonderful taste which makes every meal such a pleasure, then I am against it!"

What we need, perhaps, is more: not only drawing the line distinguishing the good from the bad Israel, but an authentic act of changing the very coordinates of the present situation. The former Israeli prime minister Yitzhak Rabin took the first big step in this direction when he recognised the PLO as the legitimate representative of the Palestinians and thus the only true partner in negotiations. When Rabin announced the reversal of the Israeli politics of "no negotiations with the PLO, a terrorist organisation," and pronounced the simple words "let us end with this charade of negotiating with the Palestinians with no public links to the PLO and start talking with our real partners," the Middle East situation changed overnight. Therein resides the effect of a true political act: it renders the unthinkable thinkable. Although a Labour politician, Rabin thus accomplished a gesture that characterises conservative politicians at their best: only a de Gaulle could grant Algeria independence; only a conservative like Nixon could establish relations with China.[16]

So what would constitute an *act* of this kind for the Arabs today? To do what Ed Norton does in *Fight Club*: to first *strike back at themselves*–to stop putting all the blame on Jews, as if the Zionist expansion in Palestine is the origin and symbolic stand-in for all Arab misfortunes, so that the victory over Israel is the sine qua non of Arab self-assertion. The Palestinians who claim that the liberation of their territory from Israeli occupation will give an impetus to the democratisation of the Arab world have got it wrong. Things are the other way round. One should *start* by openly confronting corrupted clerical and military regimes from Syria to Saudi Arabia which use the Israeli occupation to legitimise themselves. The paradox is that the very focus on Israel is the reason the Arabs are losing the battle. The basic meaning of *jihad* in Islam is not war against the external enemy, but the effort of inner purification. The struggle is against one's own moral failure and weakness. So perhaps Muslims should more actively practise the passage from the publicly best-known meaning to the true meaning of *jihad*. All three main agents of the War on Terror (the U.S. after 9/11, Israel, the Arabs) see themselves as victims and use their victimhood to legitimise their expansionist politics. There is a way in which 9/11 came at the right moment to justify America's aggressive military expansionism: now that we are also victims, we can defend ourselves and strike back. The U.S.–Israel alliance, this strange association of the most religious (developed) nation in the world insisting on the separation of religion and state, and the most irreligious people in the world existing on the religious nature of their state, can thus present itself as an axis of victims.

So to the big question: what would be the truly radical ethico-political act today in the Middle East? For both Israelis and Arabs, it would consist in the gesture of renouncing (political) control of Jerusalem, that is, of endorsing the transformation of the Old Town of Jerusalem into an extra-state place of religious worship controlled (temporarily) by some neutral international force. What both sides should accept is that by renouncing political control of Jerusalem, they are effectively renouncing nothing. They are *gaining* the elevation of Jerusalem into a genuinely extra-political, sacred site. What they would lose is precisely and only what already, in itself, deserves to be lost: the reduction of religion to a stake in political power play. This would be a true event in the Middle East, the explosion of true political universality in the Paulinian sense of "there are for us no Jews and no Palestinians." Each of the two sides would have to realise that this renunciation of the ethnically "pure" nation-state is a liberation for themselves, not simply a sacrifice to be made for the other.

Let's go back to the story about the Caucasian chalk circle on which Brecht based one of his late plays. In ancient times, somewhere in the Caucasus, a biological mother and a stepmother appealed to a judge to decide to which one of them the child belonged. The judge drew a chalk circle on the ground, placed the baby in the middle and told the two women to take one arm each; the child would belong to the one who pulled him out of the circle first. When the real mother saw that the child was hurt by being pulled in opposite directions, she released her hold out of compassion. Of course, the judge gave the child to her, claiming that she displayed true maternal love. Along these lines, one could imagine a Jerusalem chalk circle. The one who truly loves Jerusalem would rather let it go than see it torn apart by strife. Of course, the supreme irony here is that this Brechtian anecdote is a variation on the judgment of King Solomon from the Old Testament, who, acknowledging there was no just way to resolve the maternal dilemma, proposed a two-state solution: the child should be cut in two, each mother getting half. The true mother, of course, gave up her claim to the child.

What the Jews and the Palestinians share is the fact that a diasporic existence is part of their lives, part of their very identity. What if they were to come together on *this* ground: not on the ground of occupying, possessing, or dividing the same territory, but of both keeping their shared territory open as a refuge for those condemned to wander? What if Jerusalem became not their place, but a place for those with no place? This shared solidarity is the only ground for a true reconciliation: the realisation that in fighting the other, one fights what is most vulnerable in one's own life. Which is why, with full awareness of how serious the conflict and its potential consequences are, one should insist more than ever that we are dealing with a *false* conflict, with a conflict which blurs and mystifies the true front line.

The Anonymous Religion of Atheism

In the raging Muslim crowd, we stumble upon the limit of multicultural liberal tolerance, of its propensity to self-blame and its effort to "understand" the other. The Other here has become a real other, real in his hatred. Here is the paradox of tolerance at its purest: how far should tolerance for intolerance go? All the beautiful, politically correct, liberal formulas on how the Muhammad caricatures were insulting and insensitive, but violent reactions to them are also unacceptable, about how freedom brings responsibility and should not be abused, show their limitation here. What is this famous "freedom with responsibility" if not a new version of the good old paradox of forced choice? You are given freedom of choice, on condition that you make the right choice; you are given freedom, on condition that you will not really use it.

How, then, are we to break this vicious circle of endless oscillation between pro and contra which brings tolerant reason to a debilitating standstill? There is only one way: to reject the very terms in which the problem is posed. As Gilles Deleuze repeatedly emphasised, there are not only right and wrong solutions to problems, there are also right and wrong problems. To perceive the problem as one of the right measure between respect for the other versus our own freedom of expression is in itself a mystification. No wonder that upon closer analysis, the two opposing poles reveal their secret solidarity. The language of respect is the language of liberal tolerance: respect only has meaning as respect for those with whom I do *not* agree. When offended Muslims demand respect for their otherness, they are accepting the frame of the liberal-tolerant discourse. On the other hand, blasphemy is not only an attitude of hatred, of trying to hit the other where it hurts most, which is at the fundamental core of his belief. Blasphemy is, in the strict sense, a religious problem: it only works within the contours of a religious space.

What lurks at the horizon if we avoid this path is the nightmarish prospect of a society regulated by a perverse pact between religious fundamentalists and the politically correct preachers of tolerance and respect for the other's beliefs: a society immobilised by the concern for not hurting the other, no matter how cruel and superstitious this other is and in which individuals are engaged in regular rituals of "witnessing" their victimisation. When I visited the University of Champaign in Illinois, I was taken to a restaurant where the menu offered Tuscany fries. When I asked friends about this they explained that the owner wanted to appear patriotic apropos the French opposition to the U.S. attack on Iraq, so he followed the U.S. Congress and renamed French fries "freedom fries." However, the progressive members of the faculty (the majority of his customers) threatened to boycott his place if freedom fries remained on the menu. The owner didn't want to lose his customers, but still wanted to appear patriotic, so he invented a new name, "Tuscany fries." This had the added advantage of sounding European, and also echoing the vogue of idyllic films about Tuscany.

In a move similar to that of the U.S. Congress, Iranian authorities ordered bakeries to change the name "Danish pastry" to "rose of Muhammad." It would be nice to live in a world where the U.S. Congress would change the name of French fries to Muhammad fries, and the Iranian authorities transform Danish pastries into roses of freedom. But the prospect of tolerance makes one imagine that our store and restaurant menus will fill up with versions of Tuscany fries.

Over these last years, a public debate has raged in my native Slovenia: should the Muslims, mostly immigrant workers from ex-Yugoslav republics, be allowed to build a mosque in Ljubljana, the capital? While conservatives opposed the mosque for cultural, political, and even architectural reasons, the weekly journal *Mladina* was most consistent and vociferous in its support for the mosque, in line with its general support for the civil and social rights of people from other ex-Yugoslav republics. Not surprisingly, in line with its libertarian attitude, *Mladina* was also the only paper to reprint the Muhammad caricatures. And conversely, those who displayed the greatest "understanding" of the violent Muslim protest were the very ones who regularly expressed their concern for Christian Europe.

The parallel these conservatives evoked was with a scandal in Slovenia a couple of years ago. A rock group, Strelnikoff, printed a poster announcing their concert. It showed a classical painting of Mary and baby Jesus, but with a twist. In her lap, Mary holds a rat instead of her baby. The point of the parallel was, of course, to reprimand the caricatures mocking Christianity, alongside the Muhammad ones. Simultaneously the conservatives took the opportunity to note the difference in the reactions of the concerned religious communities as an argument for the difference of civilisations. Europe emerged as undoubtedly superior since we, Christians, limited ourselves to verbal protests, while the Muslims resorted to killing and burning.

Such strange alliances confront the European Muslim community with a difficult choice which encapsulates their paradoxical position: the only political grouping which does not reduce them to second-class citizens and allows them the space to deploy their religious identity are the "godless" atheist liberals, while those who are closest to their religious social practice, their Christian mirror-image, are their greatest political enemies. The paradox is that not those who first published the caricatures, but those who, out of solidarity with freedom of expression, reprinted the Muhammad caricatures, are their only true allies.

Marx's analysis of the political imbroglio of the French Revolution of 1848 comes to mind. The ruling Party of Order was the coalition of the two royalist wings, the Bourbons and the Orléanists. The two parties were, by definition, unable to find a common denominator at the level of royalism, since one cannot be a royalist in general, one can only support a determinate royal house. The only way for the two to unite was under the banner of the "anonymous kingdom of the Republic." In other words, the only way to be a royalist in general is to be a republican.[17] The same holds true for religion. One cannot be religious in general. One can only believe in some god(s) to the detriment of others. The failure of all the efforts to unite religions proves that the only way to be religious in general is under the banner of the "anonymous religion of atheism." As the fate of the Muslim communities in the West demonstrates, it is only under this banner that they can thrive.

There is thus a kind of poetic justice in the fact that the all-Muslim outcry against godless Denmark was immediately followed by heightened violence between Sunnis and Shi'ites, the two Muslim factions in Iraq. The lesson of all totalitarianisms is writ large here: the fight against the external enemy sooner or later always turns into an inner split and the fight against the inner enemy.

After all the recent arguments proclaiming the "post-secular" return of the religious, the limits of disenchantment, and the need to rediscover the sacred, perhaps what we truly need is a dose of good old atheism. The outrage caused by the Muhammad cartoons in Muslim communities may seem to provide one more proof that religious beliefs are a force to be reckoned with. Deplorable as the violence of the Muslim crowds may be, it seems to underline the fact that reckless and cynical Western libertarians must also learn their lesson from it: here are the limits of secular disenchantment. Or so we are told.

But is this really the lesson to be learned from the mob's killing, looting, and burning on behalf of religion? For a long time we have been told that without religion, we are mere egotistic animals fighting for our lot, our only morality that of the wolf pack, and that only religion can elevate us to a higher spiritual level. Today, as religion emerges as the main source of murderous violence around the world, one grows tired of the constant assurances that Christian, Muslim, or Hindu fundamentalists are only abusing and perverting the noble spiritual message of their creed. Isn't it time to restore the dignity of atheism, perhaps our only chance for peace? As a rule, where religiously inspired violence is concerned, we put the blame on violence itself: it is the violent or "terrorist" political agent who "misuses" a noble religion, so the goal becomes to retrieve the authentic core of a religion from its political instrumentalisation. What, however, if one should take the risk of inverting this relationship? What if what appears as a moderating force, compelling us to control our violence, is its secret instigator? What if, then, instead of renouncing violence, one were to renounce religion, including its secular reverberations such as Stalinist communism with its reliance on the historical big Other, and to pursue violence on its own, assuming full responsibility for it, without any cover-up in some figure of the big Other?

It is often claimed that every contemporary ethical dispute is really a debate between Charles Darwin and the Pope. On the one side there is secular (im)morality, which finds it acceptable and desirable ruthlessly to use and sacrifice individuals. On the other, there is Christian morality, which asserts that every single human being has an immortal soul and is thus sacred. In this context it's interesting to note how, after the outbreak of the First World War, some social Darwinians were pacifists on account of their anti-egalitarian Darwinism; Ernst Haeckel, the leading proponent of social Darwinism, opposed the war because in it, the wrong people were killed: "The stronger, healthier, more normal the young man is, the greater is the prospect for him to be murdered by the needle gun, cannons, and other similar instruments of culture."[18] The problem was that the weak and sick were not allowed into the army. They were left free to have children and thus lead the nation into biological decline. One of the solutions envisaged was to force everyone to serve in the army and then, in battle, ruthlessly use the weak and sick as cannon fodder in suicidal attacks.

What complicates all this today is that mass killings are more and more legitimated in religious terms, while pacifism is predominantly atheist. It is the very belief in a higher divine goal which allows us to instrumentalise individuals, while atheism admits no such goal and thus refuses all forms of sacred sacrificing. No wonder, then, that as AP reported on 12 November 2006, Elton John, while admiring the teachings of Christ and other spiritual leaders, opposes all organised religions. "I think religion has always tried to turn hatred towards gay people," Elton said in the *Observer* newspaper's music supplement. "Religion promotes the hatred and spite against gays . . . From my point of view, I would ban religion completely. Organised religion doesn't seem to work. It turns people into really hateful lemmings and it's not really compassionate." Religious leaders had also failed to do anything about tensions and conflicts around the world. "Why aren't they having a conclave? Why aren't they coming together?" he asked.

The predominance of religiously (or ethnically) justified violence can be accounted for by the very fact that we live in an era that perceives itself as post-ideological. Since great public causes can no longer be mobilised to ground mass violence (i.e., war), since our hegemonic ideology calls on us to enjoy life and to realise our own selves, it is difficult for the majority to overcome their revulsion at torturing and killing another human being. The large majority of people are spontaneously "moral": killing another human being is deeply traumatic for them. So, in order to make them do it, a larger "sacred" cause is needed, which makes petty individual concerns about killing seem trivial. Religion or ethnic belonging fits this role perfectly. Of course there are cases of pathological atheists who are able to commit mass murder just for pleasure, just for the sake of it, but they are rare exceptions. The majority needs to be "anaesthetised" against their elementary sensitivity to the other's suffering. For this, a sacred cause is needed.

More than a century ago, in his *Brothers Karamazov*, Dostoevsky warned against the dangers of godless moral nihilism: *"If God doesn't exist, then everything is permitted."* The French "new philosopher" André Glucksmann applied Dostoevsky's critique of godless nihilism to 9/11, as the title of his book–*Dostoevsky in Manhattan*–suggests.[19] He couldn't have been more wrong: the lesson of today's terrorism is that if there *is* a God, then everything, even blowing up hundreds of innocent bystanders, is permitted to those who claim to act directly on behalf of God, as the instruments of his will, since clearly a direct link to God justifies our violation of any "merely human" constraints and considerations. The "godless" Stalinist communists are the ultimate proof of it: everything was permitted to them since they perceived themselves as direct instruments of their divinity, the Historical Necessity of Progress towards Communism.

The formula of the fundamentalist religious suspension of the ethical was proposed by Augustine, who wrote: "Love God and do as you please." Alternately, this becomes "Love, and do whatever you want," since from the Christian perspective, the two ultimately amount to the same. God, after all, is love. The catch, of course, is that if you really love God, you will want what he wants—what pleases him will please you, and what displeases him will make you miserable. So it is not that you can just do whatever you want: your love for God, if true, guarantees that in what you want to do you will follow the highest ethical standards. This is a little bit like the proverbial joke: "My fiancée is never late for an appointment, because when she is late, she is no longer my fiancée." If you love God, you can do whatever you want, because when you do something evil, this is in itself a proof that you do not really love God . . . However, the ambiguity persists, since there is no guarantee, external to your belief, of what God really wants you to do. In the absence of any ethical standards external to your belief in and love for God, the danger is always lurking that you will use your love of God as the legitimisation of the most horrible deeds.

In the course of the Crusade of King St. Louis, Yves le Breton reported how he once encountered an old woman who wandered down the street with a dish full of fire in her right hand and a bowl full of water in her left hand. Asked what she was doing, she answered that with the fire she would burn up Paradise until nothing remained of it, and with the water she would put out the fires of Hell until nothing remained of them, "Because I want no one to do good in order to receive the reward of Paradise, or from fear of Hell; but solely out of love for God."[20] The only thing to add to this is: so why not erase God himself and just do good for the sake of it? No wonder that, today, this properly Christian ethical stance survives mostly in atheism.

Fundamentalists do (what they perceive as) good deeds in order to fulfil God's will and to deserve salvation; atheists do them simply because it is the right thing to do. Is this also not our most elementary experience of morality? When I do a good deed, I do not do it with a view to gaining God's favour, I do it because I cannot do otherwise—if I were not to do it, I would not be able to look at myself in the mirror. A moral deed is by definition its own reward. The eighteenth-century economist-philosopher David Hume, a believer, made this point in a very poignant way when he wrote that the only way to show a true respect for God is to act morally while ignoring God's existence.

The history of European atheism, from its Greek and Roman origins in Lucretius's *De rerum natura* to modern classics like Spinoza, offers a lesson in dignity and courage. Much more than with occasional outbursts of hedonism, it is marked by the awareness of the bitter outcome of every human life, since there is no higher authority watching over our fates and guaranteeing the happy outcome. At the same time, atheists strive to formulate the message of joy which comes not from escaping reality, but from accepting it and creatively finding one's place in it. What makes this materialist tradition unique is the way it combines the humble awareness that we are not masters of the universe, but just parts of a much larger whole exposed to contingent twists of fate, with a readiness to accept the heavy burden of responsibility for what we make out of our lives. With the threat of unpredictable catastrophe looming from all sides, isn't this an attitude needed more than ever in our own times?

A couple of years ago a particular debate raged in Europe: should Christianity be mentioned as the key component of European heritage in the preamble to the draft of the European constitution? A compromise was worked out in which Christianity was listed along with Judaism, Islam, and the legacy of Antiquity. But where was modern Europe's most precious legacy, that of atheism? What makes modern Europe unique is that it is the first and only civilisation in which atheism is a fully legitimate option, not an obstacle to any public post. This is most emphatically a European legacy worth fighting for.

While the true atheist has no need whatsoever to boost his own stance by way of shocking the believer with blasphemous statements, he also refuses to reduce the problem of the Muhammad caricatures to one of respect for others' beliefs. Respect for others' beliefs as the highest value can mean only one of two things: either we treat the other in a patronising way and avoid hurting him in order not to ruin his illusions, or we adopt the relativist stance of multiple "regimes of truth," disqualifying as violent imposition any clear insistence on truth. What, however, about submitting Islam— together with all other religions—to a respectful, but for that reason no less ruthless, critical analysis? This, and only this, is the way to show true respect for Muslims: to treat them as serious adults responsible for their beliefs.

Molto adagio–Andante

TOLERANCE AS AN IDEOLOGICAL CATEGORY

The Culturalisation of Politics

Why are so many problems today perceived as problems of intolerance, rather than as problems of inequality, exploitation, or injustice? Why is the proposed remedy tolerance, rather than emancipation, political struggle, even armed struggle? The immediate answer lies in the liberal multiculturalist's basic ideological operation: the "culturalisation of politics." Political differences–differences conditioned by political inequality or economic exploitation–are naturalised and neutralised into "cultural" differences, that is, into different "ways of life" which are something given, something that cannot be overcome. They can only be "tolerated." This demands a response in the terms Walter Benjamin offers: *from culturalisation of politics to politicisation of culture*. The cause of this culturalisation is the retreat, the failure of direct political solutions such as the Welfare State or various socialist projects. Tolerance is their post-political ersatz.[1]

It was political scientist Samuel Huntington who proposed the most successful formula of this "culturalisation of politics" by locating the main source of today's conflicts in the "clash of civilisations," which one is tempted to call the Huntington's disease of our time. As Huntington put it, after the end of the Cold War, the "iron curtain of ideology" has been replaced by the "velvet curtain of culture."[2] Huntington's dark vision of the "clash of civilisations" may appear to be the very opposite of Francis Fukuyama's bright prospect of the end of history in the guise of a worldwide liberal democracy. What can be more different from Fukuyama's pseudo-Hegelian idea of the "end of history"–the ultimate formula of the best possible social order has been found in capitalist liberal democracy, so there is now no space for further conceptual progress; there are only empirical obstacles to be overcome[3]–than Huntington's "clash of civilisations" as the main political struggle in the twenty-first century? *The "clash of civilisations" is politics at the end of history.*

The basic opposition on which the entire liberal vision relies is that between those who are ruled by culture, totally determined by the lifeworld into which they are born, and those who merely "enjoy" their culture, who are elevated above it, free to choose it. This brings us to the next paradox: the ultimate source of barbarism is culture itself, one's direct identification with a particular culture, which renders one intolerant towards other cultures. The basic opposition here is that between the collective and the individual: culture is by definition collective and particular, parochial, exclusive of other cultures, while–next paradox–it is the individual who is universal, the site of universality, insofar as she extricates herself from and elevates herself above her particular culture. Since, however, every individual has to be somehow particularised, has to dwell in a particular lifeworld, the only way to resolve this deadlock is to split the individual into universal and particular, public and private (where "private" covers both the safe haven of family *and* the non-state public sphere of civil society (economy)).

In liberalism, culture survives, but as privatised: as a way of life, a set of beliefs and practices, not the public network of norms and rules. Culture is thus literally transubstantiated: the same sets of beliefs and practices change from the binding power of a collective into an expression of personal and private idiosyncrasies. Insofar as culture itself is the source of barbarism and intolerance, the inevitable conclusion is that the only way to overcome intolerance and violence is to extricate the core of the subject's being, its universal essence, from culture: in her core, the subject has to be *kulturlos*.[4] The philosophical underpinning of this ideology of the universal liberal subject is the Cartesian subject, especially in its Kantian version. This subject is conceived of as capable of stepping outside his particular cultural/social roots and asserting his full autonomy and universality–the grounding experience of Descartes's position of universal doubt is precisely a "multicultural" experience of how one's own tradition is no better than what appears to us the "eccentric" traditions of others:

[...] I had been taught, even in my College days, that there is nothing imaginable so strange or so little credible that it has not been maintained by one philosopher or other, and I further recognized in the course of my travels that all those whose sentiments are very contrary to ours are yet not necessarily barbarians or savages, but may be possessed of reason in as great or even a greater degree than ourselves.[5]

This is why, for a Cartesian philosopher, ethnic roots, national identity, and so on are simply *not a category of truth.* To put it in precise Kantian terms, when we reflect upon our ethnic roots, we engage in a *private use of reason,* constrained by contingent dogmatic presuppositions, that is, we act as "immature" individuals, not as free human beings who dwell in the dimension of the universality of reason. The opposition between Kant and Richard Rorty with regard to this distinction of public and private is rarely noted, but none the less crucial: they both sharply distinguish between the two domains, but in opposed ways. For Rorty, the great contemporary liberal if there ever was one, the private is the space of our idiosyncrasies, where creativity and wild imagination rule and moral considerations are (almost) suspended, while the public is the space of social interaction, where we should obey the rules so that we do not hurt others; in other words, the private is the space of irony, while the public is the space of solidarity.

For Kant, however, the public space of "world-civil-society" designates the paradox of the universal singularity, of a singular subject who, in a kind of short-circuit, by-passing the mediation of the particular, directly participates in the universal. This is what Kant, in the famous passage of his "What is Enlightenment?" means by "public" as opposed to "private." "Private" is not one's individual as opposed to communal ties, but the very communal-institutional order of one's particular identification; while "public" is the transnational universality of the exercise of one's reason. The paradox of the underlying formula "think freely, but obey!" (which, of course, poses a series of problems of its own, since it also relies on the distinction between the "performative" level of social authority, and the level of free thinking where performativity is suspended) is thus that one participates in the universal dimension of the "public" sphere precisely as a singular individual extracted from or even opposed to one's substantial communal identification–one is truly universal only when radically singular, in the interstices of communal identities. It is Kant who should be read here as the critic of Rorty. In his vision of the public space of the unconstrained free exercise of reason, he asserts the dimension of emancipatory universality *outside* the confines of one's social identity, of one's position within the order of (social) being. This is the dimension missing in Rorty.

The Effective Universality

It is easy to render this liberal notion of tolerance problematic, and to render palpable the violence that sustains it. Firstly, it is not truly universal, *kulturlos,* without culture. Since, in our societies, a gendered division of labour still predominates which confers a male twist on basic liberal categories (autonomy, public activity, competition) and relegates women to the private sphere of family solidarity, liberalism itself, in its opposition of private and public, harbours male dominance. Furthermore, it is only modern Western capitalist culture for which autonomy and individual freedom stand higher than collective solidarity, connection, responsibility for dependent others, the duty to respect the customs of one's community. Liberalism itself thus privileges a certain culture: the modern Western one. As to freedom of choice, liberalism is also marked by a strong bias. It is intolerant when individuals of other cultures are not given freedom of choice–as is evident in issues such as clitoridectomy, child brideship, infanticide, polygamy, and incest. However, it ignores the tremendous pressure which, for example, compels women in our liberal society to undergo such procedures as plastic surgery, cosmetic implants, and Botox injections in order to remain competitive in the sex market.

The liberal idea of a "free choice" thus always gets caught in a deadlock. If the subject wants it, he or she can opt for the parochial tradition into which they were born, but they have first to be presented with alternatives and then make a free choice among them. Amish adolescents, on the other hand, are formally given a free choice, but the conditions they find themselves in while they are making the choice make the choice unfree. In order for them to have a genuine free choice, they would have to be properly informed on all the options and educated in them. But the only way to do this would be to extract them from their embeddedness in the Amish community and Americanise them.

The limitations of the standard liberal attitude towards Muslim women wearing a veil are visible here, too. Women are permitted to wear the veil if this is their free choice and not an option imposed on them by their husbands or family. However, the moment women wear a veil to exercise a free individual choice, say in order to realise their own spirituality, the meaning of wearing a veil changes completely. It is no longer a sign of their belonging to the Muslim community, but an expression of their idiosyncratic individuality. The difference is the same as the one between a Chinese farmer eating Chinese food because his village has been doing so since time immemorial, and a citizen of a Western megalopolis deciding to go and have dinner at a local Chinese restaurant. This is why, in our secular, choice-based societies, people who maintain a substantial religious belonging are in a subordinate position. Even if they are allowed to maintain their belief, this belief is "tolerated" as their idiosyncratic personal choice or opinion. The moment they present it publicly as what it is for them, say a matter of substantial belonging, they are accused of "fundamentalism." What this means is that the "subject of free choice" in the Western "tolerant" multicultural sense can emerge only as the result of an extremely *violent* process of being torn out of a particular lifeworld, of being cut off from one's roots.

One should always bear in mind the hugely liberating aspect of this violence which makes us experience our own cultural background as contingent. Let us not forget that liberalism emerged in Europe after the catastrophe of the Thirty Years War between Catholics and Protestants. It was an answer to the pressing question of how people who differ in their fundamental religious allegiances could coexist. It demanded from citizens more than a condescending tolerance of diverging religions, more than tolerance as a temporary compromise. It demanded that we respect other religions not *in spite of* our innermost religious convictions but *on account of* them–respect for others is a proof of true belief. This attitude is best expressed by Abu Hanifa, the great eighth-century Muslim intellectual: "Difference of opinion in the community is a token of Divine mercy."[6] It is only within this ideological space that one can experience one's identity as something contingent and discursively "constructed." To cut a long story short, philosophically, there is no Judith Butler, or her theory of gender identity as performatively enacted, without the Cartesian subject. Whatever else one can accuse liberal multiculturalism of, one should at least admit that it is profoundly anti-"essentialist": it is its barbarian Other which is perceived as essentialist *and thereby false*. Fundamentalism "naturalises" or "essentialises" historically conditioned contingent traits. To modern Europeans, other civilisations are caught in their specific culture, while modern Europeans are flexible, constantly changing their presuppositions.

"Postcolonial" critics like to emphasise the insensitivity of liberalism to its own limitation: in defending human rights, it tends to impose its own version of them onto others. However, the self-reflexive sensitivity to one's own limitation can only emerge against the background of the notions of autonomy and rationality promoted by liberalism. One can, of course, argue that, in a way, the Western situation is even worse because in it oppression itself is obliterated and masked as free choice. (What are you complaining for? YOU chose to do this.) Our freedom of choice effectively often functions as a mere formal gesture of consent to our own oppression and exploitation. However, Hegel's lesson that form matters is important here: form has an autonomy and efficiency of its own. So when we compare a Third World woman, forced to undergo clitoridectomy or promised in marriage as a small child, with the First World woman "free to choose" painful cosmetic surgery, the form of freedom matters–it opens up a space for critical reflection.

Furthermore, the counterpart of the dismissal of other cultures as intolerant or barbarian is the all-too-easy admission of their superiority. Remember how many British colonisers in India admired the depth of Indian spirituality, out of reach to us in the West on account of our obsession with rationality and material wealth. Isn't one of the topoi of Western liberalism the elevation of the Other as leading a life that is more harmonious, organic, less competitive, and aiming at cooperation rather than domination? Linked to this is another operation: blindness to oppression on behalf of "respect" for the Other's culture. Even freedom of choice is often evoked here in a perverted way: those people have chosen their way of life, inclusive of burning widows, and deplorable and repulsive as it appears to us, we should respect their choice.

The "radical" postcolonial critique of liberalism thus remains at the standard Marxist level of denouncing false universality, of showing how a position that presents itself as neutral-universal effectively privileges a certain (heterosexual, male, Christian) culture. More precisely, such a stance is contained within the standard postmodern, anti-essentialist position, a kind of political version of Foucault's notion of sex as generated by the multitude of sexual practices: here "man," the bearer of human rights, is generated by a set of political practices which materialise citizenship. Human rights emerge as a false ideological universality which masks and legitimises the concrete politics of Western imperialism and domination, military interventions, and neocolonialism. The question is, does this suffice to constitute a critique?

The Marxist symptomal reading can convincingly demonstrate the particular content that gives the specific bourgeois ideological spin to the notion of human rights: universal human rights are effectively the rights of white male property owners to exchange freely on the market and exploit workers and women, as well as exert political domination. The identification of the particular content that hegemonises the universal form is, however, only half of the story. Its other, crucial half consists in asking a much more difficult supplementary question, that of the emergence of the very form of universality. How and in what specific historical conditions does abstract universality itself become a "fact of (social) life"? In what conditions do individuals experience themselves as subjects of universal human rights? This is the point of Marx's analysis of commodity fetishism: in a society in which commodity exchange predominates, individuals themselves, in their daily lives, relate to themselves, as well as to the objects they encounter, as to contingent embodiments of abstract-universal notions. What I am, my concrete social or cultural background, is experienced as contingent, since what ultimately defines me is the abstract universal capacity to think and/or to work. Any object that can satisfy my desire is experienced as contingent, since my desire is conceived as an abstract formal capacity, indifferent towards the multitude of particular objects that might–but never fully do–satisfy it. The modern notion of a profession implies that I experience myself as an individual who is not directly "born into" his social role. What I will become depends on the interplay between the contingent social circumstances and my free choice. In that sense, the contemporary individual has a profession. He is an electrician or professor or waiter. But it is meaningless to claim that a medieval serf was a peasant by profession. The crucial point here is, again, that in certain specific social conditions of commodity exchange and global market economy, "abstraction" becomes a direct feature of actual social life. It impacts on the way concrete individuals behave and relate to their fate and to their social surroundings. Marx shares Hegel's insight into how universality becomes "for itself" only insofar as individuals no longer fully identify the kernel of their being with their particular social situation. An attendant circumstance is that these very individuals experience themselves as forever "out of joint" with regard to this situation: the concrete, effective existence of universality produces an individual without a proper place in the global edifice. In a given social structure, universality becomes "for itself" only in those individuals who lack a proper place in it. The mode of appearance of an abstract universality, its entering into actual existence, thus produces violence: it violently disrupts a preceding organic poise.

It is no longer enough to make the old Marxist point about the gap between the ideological appearance of the universal legal form and the particular interests that effectively sustain it–as is so common among politically correct critics on the left. The counter-argument that the form is never a "mere" form, but involves a dynamic of its own which leaves traces in the materiality of social life, made by theoreticians such as Claude

Lefort and Jacques Rancière, is fully valid.[7] After all, the "formal freedom" of the bourgeois sets in motion the process of altogether "material" political demands and practices, from trade unions to feminism. Rancière rightly emphasises the radical *ambiguity* of the Marxist notion of the gap between formal democracy, with its discourse of the rights of man and political freedom, and the economic reality of exploitation and domination. This gap between the "appearance" of equality-freedom and the social reality of economic and cultural differences can be interpreted in two ways: either the standard symptomatic way, according to which the form of universal rights, equality, freedom, and democracy is just a necessary but illusory expression of its concrete social content, the universe of exploitation and class domination; or in the much more subversive sense of a tension in which the "appearance" of *égaliberté* is precisely *not* a "mere appearance," but has a power of its own. This power allows it to set in motion the process of the re-articulation of actual socio-economic relations by way of their progressive "politicisation": Why shouldn't women also vote? Why shouldn't conditions at the workplace also be of public political concern? And so on. One is tempted here to use that old Levi-Straussian term "symbolic efficiency": the appearance of *égaliberté* is a symbolic fiction which, as such, possesses an actual efficiency of its own. One should resist the cynical temptation of reducing it to a mere illusion that conceals a different actuality. That would be to fall into the trap of the old Stalinist hypocrisy which mocked "merely formal" bourgeois freedom: if it was so merely formal and didn't disturb the true relations of power, why then didn't the Stalinist regime allow it? Why was it so afraid of it?

The key moment of any theoretical–and indeed ethical, political, and, as Badiou demonstrated, even aesthetic–struggle is *the rise of universality out of the particular lifeworld.* The commonplace according to which we are all thoroughly grounded in a particular, contingent lifeworld, so that all universality is irreducibly coloured by and embedded in that lifeworld, needs to be turned round. The authentic moment of discovery, the breakthrough, occurs when a properly universal dimension *explodes from within a particular context and becomes "for-itself," and is directly experienced as universal.* This universality-for-itself is not simply external to or above its particular context: it is inscribed within it. It perturbs and affects it from within, so that the identity of the particular is split into its particular and its universal aspects. Surely Marx already pointed out how the true problem with Homer was not to explain the roots of his epics in early Greek society, but to account for the fact that, although clearly rooted in their historical context, they were able to transcend their historical origin and speak to all epochs. Perhaps the most elementary hermeneutic test of the greatness of a work of art is its ability to survive being torn from its original context. In the case of truly great art, each epoch reinvents and rediscovers it. There is a romantic Shakespeare and a realist Shakespeare.

Richard Wagner's operas provide another example. Recent historicist work tries to bring out the contextual "true meaning" of various Wagnerian characters and topics: the pale Hagen is really a masturbating Jew;

Amfortas's wound is really syphilis, and so on. Wagner, the argument goes, was mobilising historical codes known to everyone in his own time: when a person stumbles, sings in cracking high tones, or makes nervous gestures, "everyone" then knew this was a Jew. Thus Mime from *Siegfried* is a caricature of a Jew. The illness in the groin caught from having intercourse with an "impure" woman was, because woman indicates syphilis, an obsession in the second half of the nineteenth century, so it was clear to everyone that Amfortas really contracted syphilis from Kundry. The first problem with such readings is that even if accurate, the insights garnered do not contribute much to a pertinent understanding of the work. Indeed, historicist commonplaces can blur our contact with art. In order properly to grasp *Parsifal,* one needs to *abstract* from such historical trivia, *decontextualise* the work, tear it out of the context in which it was originally embedded. There is more truth in *Parsifal*'s formal structure, which allows for different historical contextualisations, than in its original context. Nietzsche, Wagner's great critic, was the first to perform such a decontextualisation, proposing a new figure of Wagner: no longer Wagner as the poet of Teutonic mythology, of bombastic heroic grandeur, but the "miniaturist" Wagner, the Wagner of hystericised femininity, of delicate passages, of bourgeois family decadence.

Along the same lines, Nietzsche was repeatedly reinvented throughout the twentieth century: the conservative-heroic proto-fascist Nietzsche became the French Nietzsche and then the cultural-studies Nietzsche. Convincing historical analysis can easily show

how Nietzsche's theory was embedded in his particular political experience. His virulent attack on the "revolt of the slaves" was triggered by the Paris Commune. But this in no way contradicts the fact that there is more truth in the "decontextualised" French Nietzsche of Deleuze and Foucault than in this historically accurate Nietzsche. The argument here is not simply pragmatic. The point to be made is not that Deleuze's reading of Nietzsche, although historically inaccurate, is more productive. It is rather that the tension between the basic universal frame of Nietzsche's thought and its particular historical contextualisation is inscribed into the very edifice of Nietzsche's thought, is part of its very identity, in the same way that the tension between the universal form of human rights and their "true meaning" at the historical moment of their inception is part of their identity.

The standard Marxist hermeneutics of unearthing the particular bias of abstract universality should thus be supplemented by its opposite: by the properly Hegelian procedure which uncovers the *universality* of what presents itself as a particular position. It's worth looking again at Marx's analysis of how, in the French Revolution of 1848, the conservative-republican Party of Order functioned as the coalition of the two branches of royalism, Orléanists and legitimists, in the "anonymous kingdom of the Republic."[8] The parliamentary deputees of the Party of Order perceived their republicanism as a mockery: in parliamentary debates, they constantly generated royalist slips of tongue and ridiculed the Republic to let it be known that their true aim was to restore the kingdom. What they were not

aware of is that they themselves were duped as to the
true social impact of their rule. What they were effectively doing was to establish the very conditions of
bourgeois republican order that they so despised–by,
for instance, guaranteeing the safety of private property. So it is not that they were royalists who were
simply wearing a republican mask, although they experienced themselves as such. It was their very inner
royalist conviction which was the deceptive front mask-
ing their true social role. In short, far from being the
hidden truth of their public republicanism, their sincere royalism was the fantasmatic support of their actual republicanism. It was what provided the passion
behind their activity.

Isn't this the very lesson of Hegel's "Cunning of
Reason"? Particularity can indeed mask universality.
The French royalists of 1848 were victims of the Cunning of Reason, blind to the universal (capitalist-
republican) interest served in their pursuit of their
particular royalist goals. They were like Hegel's *valet
de chambre* who can't see the universal dimension, so
that there are no heroes for him. More generally, an
individual capitalist thinks he is active for his own
profit, ignoring how he is serving the expanded reproduction of universal capital. It is not only that every
universality is haunted by a particular content that
taints it; it is that every particular position is haunted
by its implicit universality, which undermines it. Capitalism is not just universal in itself, it is universal for
itself, as the tremendous actual corrosive power which
undermines all particular lifeworlds, cultures, and
traditions, cutting across them, catching them in its

vortex. It is meaningless to ask "Is this universality true or a mask of particular interests?" This universality is directly actual as universality, as the negative force of mediating and destroying all particular content.

This is the moment of truth in liberalism's claim to *kulturlos* universality: capitalism, whose ideology liberalism is, effectively *is* universal, no longer rooted in a particular culture or "world." This is why Badiou recently claimed that our time is *devoid of world*: the universality of capitalism resides in the fact that capitalism is not a name for a "civilisation," for a specific cultural-symbolic world, but the name for a truly neutral economic-symbolic machine which operates with Asian values as well as with others. In that sense, Europe's worldwide triumph is its defeat, its self-obliteration. Capitalism's umbilical link to Europe has been cut. The critics of Eurocentrism who endeavour to unearth the secret European bias of capitalism fall short here: the problem with capitalism is not its secret Eurocentric bias, but the fact that it *really is universal,* a neutral matrix of social relations.

The same logic holds for the emancipatory struggle: the particular culture which tries desperately to defend its identity has to repress the universal dimension which is active at its very heart, that is, the gap between the particular (its identity) and the universal which destabilises it from within. This is why the "leave us our culture" argument fails. Within every particular culture, individuals *do* suffer, women *do* protest when forced to undergo clitoridectomy, and *these protests against the parochial constraints of one's culture are formulated from the standpoint of universality.* Actual universality is not the deep feeling that above all differences, different civilisations share the same basic values, etc.; *actual universality appears (actualises itself) as the experience of negativity, of the inadequacy-to-itself, of a particular identity.* The formula of revolutionary solidarity is not "let us tolerate our differences," it is not a pact of civilisations, but a pact of struggles which cut across civilisations, a pact between what, in each civilisation, undermines its identity from within, fights against its oppressive kernel. What unites us is the same struggle. A better formula would thus be: in spite of our differences, we can identify the basic antagonism or antagonistic struggle in which we are both caught; so let us share our *intolerance,* and join forces in the same struggle. In other words, in the emancipatory struggle, it is not the cultures in their identity which join hands, it is the repressed, the exploited and suffering, the "parts of no-part" of every culture which come together in a shared struggle.

Primo Levi was often asked whether he considered himself primarily a Jew or a human. Levi often oscillated between these two choices. The obvious solution–that precisely as a Jew, he was human, that is, one is human, one participates in universal humanity, through one's very particular ethnic identification–falls flat here. The only consistent solution is not to say that Levi was a human who happened to be a Jew, but that he was human (he participated "for himself" in the universal function of humanity) precisely and only insofar as he was uneasy with or unable fully to identify with his *Jewishness*: "being a Jew" was a problem for him, not a fact, not a safe haven to which he could withdraw.

Acheronta movebo: *The Infernal Regions*

The particular ethnic substance, our "lifeworld," which resists universality, is made up of habits. But what are habits? Every legal order or every order of explicit normativeness has to rely on a complex network of informal rules which tells us how we are to relate to explicit norms: how we are to apply them; to what extent we are to take them literally; and how and when we are allowed, even solicited, to disregard them. These informal rules make up the domain of habit. To know the habits of a society is to know the meta-rules of how to apply its explicit norms: when to use them or not use them; when to violate them; when not to use a choice which is offered; when we are effectively obliged to do something, but have to pretend that we are doing it as a free choice, as in the case of potlatch. Think of all those polite offers which are meant to be refused: it is a "habit" to refuse such offers, and anyone who accepts them commits a vulgar blunder. The same holds for many political situations in which a choice is presented *on condition that we make the right choice*: we are solemnly reminded that we can say no–but we are expected to reject this offer and enthusiastically say yes. With many sexual prohibitions, the situation is the opposite one: the explicit "no" effectively functions as the implicit injunction to get on with it, but in a discreet way!

One of the strategies of totalitarian regimes is to have legal regulations (criminal laws) so severe that, if taken literally, *everyone* is guilty of something. But then their full enforcement is withdrawn. In this way, the regime can appear merciful: "You see, if we wanted, we could have all of you arrested and condemned, but do not be afraid, we are lenient . . ." At the same time the regime wields the permanent threat of disciplining its subjects: "Do not play too much with us, remember that at any moment we can . . ." In the former Yugoslavia there was the infamous Article 133 of the penal code which could always be invoked to prosecute writers and journalists. It criminalised any text that falsely presented the achievements of the socialist revolution or that *might arouse tension and discontent among the public* for the way it dealt with political, social, or other topics. This last category is obviously not only infinitely plastic, but also conveniently self-relating: doesn't the very fact that you are accused by those in power prove the fact that you "*aroused tension and discontent among the public*"? In those years, I remember asking a Slovene politician how he justified this law. He just smiled and, with a wink, told me, "Well, we have to have some tool to discipline at our will those who annoy us." Here we have an overlap of potential total culpability (whatever you are doing *may* be a crime) and mercy (the fact that you are allowed to lead your life in peace is not a proof or consequence of your innocence, but a proof of the mercy and benevolence, of an "understanding of the realities of life," of those in power). This acts as further proof that totalitarian regimes are by definition regimes of mercy: they tolerate violations of the law, since, in the way they frame social life, violating the law, bribing, and cheating are conditions of survival.

The problem of the chaotic post-Soviet years of Yeltsin rule in Russia can be located at this level: although the legal rules were known and largely the same as under the Soviet Union, what disintegrated was the complex network of implicit, unwritten rules which sustained the entire social edifice. If in the Soviet Union you wanted to get better hospital treatment or a new apartment, if you had a complaint against the authorities, if you were summoned to court, if you wanted your child to be accepted into a top school, if a factory manager needed raw materials to be delivered on time by the state contractors, and so on, everyone knew what you really had to do. Everyone knew whom to address, whom to bribe, what you could and couldn't do.

After the collapse of Soviet power, one of the most frustrating aspects of the daily existence of ordinary people was that these unwritten rules often became blurred. People simply did not know what to do, how to react, how to relate to explicit legal regulations, what to ignore, where bribery worked. One of the functions of organised crime was to provide a kind of ersatz legality: if you owned a small business and a customer owed you money, you turned to your mafia protector, who dealt with the problem, since the state legal system was inefficient. Stabilisation under the Putin regime mostly amounts to the newly established transparency of these unwritten rules: now, again, people mostly know how to navigate the complexities of social interactions.

This underlines how the most elementary level of symbolic exchange is made up of so-called "empty gestures," offers made or meant to be rejected. Brecht gave a poignant expression to this feature in his learning plays, exemplarily in *Der Jasager,* in which the young boy is asked freely to agree with what will in any case be his fate: to be thrown into the valley. As his teacher explains it to him, it is customary to ask the victim if he agrees with his fate, but it is also customary for the victim to say yes. Belonging to a society involves a paradoxical point at which each of us is ordered freely to embrace and make of it our own choice what is, in any case, imposed on us. We all *must* love our country or our parents. This paradox of willing or choosing freely what is in any case obligatory, of maintaining the appearance that there is a free choice when there isn't one, is strictly codependent with the notion of an empty symbolic gesture, a gesture–an offer–which is meant to be rejected.

Isn't something very similar part of our everyday mores? In Japan, workers have the right to forty days' holiday every year. However, they are expected not to use this right to its full extent: implicit agreement has it that no more than half should be used. In John Irving's *A Prayer for Owen Meany,* after the little boy Owen accidentally kills the mother of his best friend, John, the narrator, he is, of course, terribly upset. To show how sorry he is, he discreetly makes John a gift of his complete collection of baseball cards, his most precious possession. Dan, John's delicate stepfather, tells him that the proper thing to do is to return the gift.

Let us imagine a more down-to-earth situation. When, after being engaged in a fierce competition for a job promotion with my closest friend, I win, the proper thing to do is to offer to withdraw, so that he will get the promotion. The proper thing for him to do is to reject my offer. This way, perhaps, our friendship can continue. What we have here is symbolic exchange at its purest: a gesture made to be rejected. The magic of symbolic exchange is that although at the end we are where we were at the beginning, there is a distinct gain for both parties in their pact of solidarity. There is a similar logic at work in the process of apologising: if I hurt someone with a rude remark, the proper thing for me to do is to offer him a sincere apology, and the proper thing for him to do is to say something like, "Thanks, I appreciate it, but I wasn't offended, I knew you didn't mean it, so you really owe me no apology!" The point is, of course, that although the final result is that no apology is needed, one has to go through the process of offering it: "you owe me no apology" can be said only after I *do* offer an apology, so that although formally nothing happens, and the offer of apology is proclaimed unnecessary, there is a gain at the end of the process and perhaps a friendship is saved.

But what if the person to whom the offer to be rejected is made actually accepts it? What if, upon being beaten in the competition, I accept my friend's offer to take the promotion instead of him? Such a situation is properly catastrophic: it causes the disintegration of the semblance of freedom that pertains to social order. This is equal to the disintegration of the social substance itself, the dissolution of social links. It is in this precise sense that revolutionary-egalitarian figures from Robespierre to John Brown are–potentially, at least–*figures without habits*: they refuse to take into account the habits that qualify the functioning of a universal rule. If all men are equal, then all men are equal and are to be effectively treated as such; if blacks are also human, they need immediately to be treated as equals.

On a less radical level, in the early 1980s a half-dissident student weekly newspaper in Yugoslavia wanted to protest against the regular but rigged "free" elections in the country. Aware of the limitations of the slogan "speak truth to power" ("the trouble with this slogan is that it ignores the fact that power will not listen and that the people already know the truth as they make clear in their jokes"), instead of directly denouncing the elections as unfair, they decided to treat them as if they *really* were free, as if their result really was not pre-ordained. On the eve of the election they printed an extra edition of their paper with a large headline: "Latest election results: Communists remain in power!" This simple intervention broke the unwritten "habit" which would have it that we all know that elections are not free, we just do not talk publicly about it . . . By treating the elections as free, they publicly reminded people of their lack of freedom.

In the second season of the TV series *Nip/Tuck*, Sean learns that the true father of his adolescent son, Matt, is Christian, his partner. His first reaction is an angry outburst. Then, in the aftermath of a failed operation to separate Siamese twins, he again accepts Chris as a partner, with a big speech at the operating table: "I will never forgive you for what you did. But Matt is too precious, the best result of our partnership, so we should not lose this . . ." This message is obvious, all too obvious. A much more elegant solution would have been for

Sean just to say: "I will never forgive you for what you did." The subjective position of this statement is already that of acceptance–this is how one talks to someone whom one has already decided to re-accept–so the problem is that Sean *says too much*. Why does he go on? This is the interesting question. Is the U.S. public too stupid? No. So why, then? What if just a sign of true re-acceptance would have been too much, too intense, so the explicit platitudes are there to water it down? Perhaps, *Nip/Tuck* being an American series, this excess can be accounted for in terms of the difference between Europe and the U.S. In Europe, the ground floor in a building is counted as 0, so that the floor above it is the first floor, while in the U.S., the first floor is at street level. In short, Americans start to count with 1, while Europeans know that 1 is already a stand-in for 0. Or to put it in more historical terms, Europeans are aware that prior to beginning a count, there has to be a "ground" of tradition, a ground which is always already given and, as such, cannot be counted, while the U.S., a land with no premodern historical tradition proper, lacks such a ground. Things begin there directly with the self-legislated freedom. The past is erased or trans-posed onto Europe.[10] This lack of ground thus has to be supplemented with excessive speech: Sean cannot rely on the symbolic ground that would guarantee that Christian will get the message without explicitly stating it.

Habits are the very stuff our identities are made of. In them, we enact and thus define what we effectively are as social beings, often in contrast with our percep-tion of what we are. In their very transparency they are the medium of social violence. Back in 1937, George Orwell set out the ambiguity of the predominant leftist attitude towards class difference:

> We all rail against class-distinctions, but very few people seriously want to abolish them. Here you come upon the important fact that every revolutionary opinion draws part of its strength from a secret conviction that nothing can be changed [. . .] So long as it is merely a question of ameliorating the worker's lot, every decent person is agreed [. . .] But unfortunately you get no further by merely wishing class-distinctions away. More exactly, it *is* necessary to wish them away, but your wish has no efficacy unless you grasp what it involves. The fact that has got to be faced is that to abolish class-distinctions means abolishing a part of yourself. Here am I, a typical member of the middle class. It is easy for me to say that I want to get rid of class-distinctions, but nearly everything I think and do is a result of class-distinctions [. . .] I have got to alter myself so completely that at the end I should hardly be recognisable as the same person.[11]

Orwell's point is that radicals invoke the need for revolutionary change as a kind of superstitious token that will achieve its opposite, *prevent* the change from really occurring. Today's academic leftist who criticises capitalist cultural imperialism is in reality horrified at the idea that his field of study might break down. It is clear to Orwell that in our ideological everyday, our predominant attitude is one of a jeering distance towards our true beliefs:

the left-wing opinions of the average "intellectual" are
mainly spurious. From pure imitativeness he jeers at
things which in fact he believes in. As one example out
of many, take the public-school code of honour, with its
"team spirit" and "Don't hit a man when he's down,"
and all the rest of that familiar bunkum. Who has not
laughed at it? Who, calling himself an "intellectual,"
would dare *not* to laugh at it? But it is a bit different
when you meet somebody who laughs at it *from the
outside*; just as we spend our lives in abusing England
but grow very angry when we hear a foreigner saying
exactly the same things [. . .] It is only when you meet
someone of a different culture from yourself that you
begin to realise what your own beliefs really are.

There is nothing "inner" in this true ideological identity
that Orwell posits. Innermost beliefs are all "out there,"
embodied in practices which reach up to the immediate
materiality of my body. My notions—of good and evil,
of pleasant and unpleasant, of funny and serious, of
ugly and beautiful—are essentially *middle-class* notions; my taste in books and food and clothes, my sense
of honour, my table manners, my turns of phrase, my
accent, even the characteristic movements of my body,
are all matters of habit. *Smell* could usefully be added to
this series. Perhaps the key difference between lower-
class and middle-class concerns lies in the way they relate to smell. For the middle class, the lower classes
smell, their members do not wash regularly enough–and
this brings us to one of the possible definitions of what
Neighbour means today: a Neighbour is one who by
definition *smells*. This is why today deodorants and

soaps are crucial–they make neighbours at least minimally tolerable: I am ready to love my neighbours . . . provided they don't smell too bad. According to a recent report, scientists in a laboratory in Venezuela, through genetic manipulations, succeeded in growing beans which, upon consumption, do not generate bad-smelling and socially embarrassing wind. So, after decaf coffee, fat-free cakes, diet Cola, and alcohol-free beer, we now get wind-free beans . . . [12]

Here we come to the "heart of darkness" of habits. Remember the numerous cases of paedophilia that shattered the Catholic Church? When its representatives insist that these cases, deplorable as they may be, are the Church's internal problem and display a great reluctance to collaborate with the police in their investigations, they are, in a way, right. The paedophilia of Catholic priests is not something that concerns merely the persons who, because of accidental reasons of private history with no relation to the Church as an institution, happened to choose the priesthood as a profession. It is a phenomenon that concerns the Catholic Church as such, that is inscribed into its very functioning as a socio-symbolic institution. It does not concern the "private" unconscious of individuals, but the "unconscious" of the institution itself: it is not something that happens because the institution has to accommodate itself to the pathological realities of libidinal life in order to survive, but something that the institution itself needs in order to reproduce itself. One can well imagine a "straight" (not paedophiliac) priest who, after years of service, gets involved in paedophilia because the very logic of the institution seduces him into it.

Such an *institutional unconscious* designates the obscene disavowed underside that, precisely as disavowed, sustains the public institution. In the army, this underside consists of the obscene sexualised rituals of fragging which sustain group solidarity. In other words, it is not simply that, for conformist reasons, the Church tries to hush up the embarrassing paedophilic scandals; in defending itself, the Church defends its innermost obscene secret. What this means is that identifying oneself with this secret side is a key constituent of the very identity of a Christian priest: if a priest seriously (not just rhetorically) denounces these scandals, he thereby excludes himself from the ecclesiastic community. He is no longer "one of us" in exactly the same way that any white Southerner in the U.S. of the 1920s who informed on the Ku Klux Klan excluded himself from his community, having betrayed its fundamental solidarity. Consequently, the answer to the Church's reluctance should be not only that we are dealing with criminal cases and that if the Church does not fully participate in their investigation, it is an accomplice after the fact. The Church as an institution should *itself* be investigated with regard to the way it systematically creates conditions for such crimes.

This obscene underground, the unconscious terrain of habits, is what is really difficult to change. This is why the motto of every radical revolution is the same as the quote from Virgil that Freud chose as the epigraph for his *Interpretation of Dreams*: *Acheronta movebo*–I will move the infernal regions. Dare to disturb the underground of the unspoken underpinnings of our everyday lives!

"Humoresque," arguably Robert Schumann's piano masterpiece, is to be read against the background of the gradual loss of the voice in his songs: it is not a simple piano piece, but a song without the vocal line, with the vocal line reduced to silence, so that all we effectively hear is the piano accompaniment. This is how one should read the famous "inner voice" (*innere Stimme*) added by Schumann in the written score as a third line between the two piano lines, higher and lower: as the vocal melodic line which remains a non-vocalised "inner voice." What we hear is a series of variations without a theme, accompaniment without a main melodic line which exists only as *Augenmusik*, music for the eyes only, in the guise of written notes. This absent melody is to be reconstructed on the basis of the fact that the first and third levels–the right- and left-hand piano lines–do not relate to each other directly, that is, their relationship is not that of an immediate mirroring. In order to account for their interconnection, one is thus compelled to (re)construct a third, "virtual" intermediate level, the melodic line, which, for structural reasons, cannot be played. Its status is that of an impossible real which can exist only in the guise of the written. Its physical presence would annihilate the two melodic lines we effectively hear in reality.

In his short essay "A Child Is Being Beaten," Freud analyses a child's fantasy of witnessing another child being severely beaten; he locates this fantasy as the last in a chain of three, the previous two being "I see my father beating a child" and "My father is beating me." The child was never conscious of the second scene, so it has to be reconstructed to provide the missing link between the first and the last scenes–like Schumann's third melodic line which is never played, but has to be reconstructed by the listener as the missing link between the two lines that one hears. Schumann brings this procedure of absent melody to an apparently absurd self-reference when, later in the same fragment of "Humoresque," he repeats the same two effectively played melodic lines, yet this time the score contains no third absent melodic line, no inner voice: what is absent here is the absent melody, or absence itself. How are we to play these notes when, at the level of what is effectively to be played, they exactly repeat the previous notes? These played notes are deprived only of what is not there, of their constitutive lack, or, to paraphrase the Bible, they lose even what they never had.[13] The true pianist should thus have the *savoir-faire* to play the existing, positive, notes in such a way that one would be able to discern the echo of the accompanying unplayed "silent" virtual notes or their absence.

Isn't this how ideology works? The explicit ideological text or practice is sustained by an unplayed series of obscene superego supplements. In Really Existing Socialism, the explicit ideology of socialist democracy was sustained by a set of implicit and unspoken, obscene injunctions and prohibitions, which taught the subject how not to take some explicit norms seriously and how to implement a set of publicly unacknowledged prohibitions. One of the strategies of dissidence in the last years of socialism was therefore precisely to take the ruling ideology more seriously and literally than it took itself by way of ignoring its virtual unwritten shadow: "You want us to practise socialist democracy? OK, here you

have it!" And when one got back from the party apparatchiks desperate hints of how this was not the way
things functioned, one simply had to ignore these hints.
This is what *acheronta movebo* as a practice of the critique of ideology means: not directly changing the explicit text of the law but, rather, intervening in its
obscene virtual supplement.

Remember how the relationship with homosexuality
in a soldiers' community operates? There are two clearly
distinct levels: explicit homosexuality is brutally attacked,
those identified as gays are ostracised, beaten up every
night, and so on. However, this explicit homophobia is
accompanied by an implicit web of homosexual innu-
endos, in-jokes, and obscene practices. The truly radical
intervention in military homophobia should therefore
not focus primarily on the explicit repression of homosexuality; it should rather "move the underground,"
disturb the implicit homosexual practices which *sustain* the explicit homophobia.

It is this obscene underground which enables us to
approach the Abu Ghraib phenomenon in a new way. In
his reaction to the photos showing Iraqi prisoners tortured and humiliated by U.S. soldiers, made public at
the end of April 2004, George Bush, as expected, emphasised how the deeds of the soldiers were isolated
crimes which do not reflect what America stands and
fights for–the values of democracy, freedom, and personal dignity. And, effectively, the very fact that the case
turned into a public scandal which put the U.S. administration in a defensive position was in itself a positive
sign. In a really "totalitarian" regime, the case would
simply have been hushed up. (In the same way, let us not

forget that the very fact that the U.S. forces did not find weapons of mass destruction is a positive sign: a truly "totalitarian" power would have done what bad cops usually do–plant the evidence and then "discover" it.)

However, a number of disturbing features complicate this simple picture. The main feature that strikes the eye is the contrast between the "standard" way prisoners were tortured in Saddam's regime and the U.S. army tortures. Under Saddam, the accent was on direct and brutal infliction of pain. The American soldiers focused on psychological humiliation. *Recording* the humiliation with a camera, with the perpetrators, a stupid grin on their faces, *included* in the picture, side by side with the twisted naked bodies of their prisoners, is an integral part of the process, in stark contrast to the secrecy of the Saddam tortures. When I saw the well-known photo of a naked prisoner with a black hood covering his head, electric cables attached to his limbs, standing on a chair in a ridiculous theatrical pose, my first reaction was that this was a shot from the latest performance-art show in Lower Manhattan. The very positions and costumes of the prisoners suggest a theatrical staging, a kind of *tableau vivant,* which cannot but bring to mind the whole spectrum of American performance art and "theatre of cruelty"–the photos of Mapplethorpe, the weird scenes in David Lynch's films, to name but two.

It is this feature that brings us to the crux of the matter: to anyone acquainted with the reality of the American way of life, the photos immediately evoked the obscene underside of U.S. popular culture–say, the initiation rituals of torture and humiliation one has to undergo in order to be accepted into a closed community. Similar photos appear at regular intervals in the U.S. press when some scandal explodes in an army unit or on a high-school campus where the initiation ritual went overboard and soldiers or students were forced to assume a humiliating pose or to perform debasing acts, such as inserting a beer bottle into their anus or being pierced by needles, while their peers looked on. Hurt here went beyond a level considered tolerable and the press were informed. (Incidentally, since Bush himself is a member of Skull and Bones, the most exclusive secret society at Yale, it would be interesting to learn which rituals he had to undergo in order to be accepted.)

Of course, the obvious difference is that in the case of such *initiation* rituals–as their very name bears witness–one undergoes them out of a free choice, fully knowing what one has to expect, and with the clear aim of the reward that awaits: of being accepted into the inner circle and–last but not least–being allowed to perform the same rituals on new members. In Abu Ghraib, the rituals were not the price to be paid by the prisoners in order to be accepted as "one of us" but, on the contrary, the very mark of their *exclusion*. But isn't the "free choice" of those undergoing the humiliating initiation rituals an exemplary case of a *false* free choice, along the lines of the worker's freedom to sell his labour? Even worse, one should recall here one of the most disgusting rituals of anti-black violence in the old American South: a black man is cornered by white thugs and then compelled to perform an aggressive gesture ("Spit into my

face, boy!"; "Say I am a shit!"), which is supposed to justify the ensuing beating or lynching. Finally, there is an
ultimate cynical message in applying to Arab prisoners
an American initiation ritual: "You want to be one of
us? OK, here's a taste of the very core of our way of
life . . ."

Rob Reiner's *A Few Good Men,* a court-martial
drama about two U.S. Marines accused of murdering
one of their fellow soldiers, comes to mind here. The
military prosecutor claims that their act was a delib-
erate murder, whereas the defence (comprising Tom
Cruise and Demi Moore–how could they fail?) succeeds
in proving that the defendants followed the so-called
Code Red, the unwritten rule of a military community
which authorises the clandestine night-time beating of
a fellow soldier who has broken the ethical standards of
the Marines. Such a code condones an act of transgression, it is "illegal," yet at the same time it reaffirms the
cohesion of the group. It has to remain under cover of
night, unacknowledged, unutterable. In public, everyone pretends to know nothing about it, or even actively
denies its existence. The climax of the film predictably
shows the outburst of Jack Nicholson, the officer who
ordered the night-time beating: his public explosion of
rage is, of course, the moment of his fall. While violating the explicit rules of community, such a code represents the "spirit of community" at its purest, exerting
the strongest pressure on individuals to enact group
identification. In contrast to the *written* and explicit
law, such an obscene superego code is essentially *spo-
ken*. While the explicit law is sustained by the dead father *qua* symbolic authority (Lacan's "Name of the

Father"), the unwritten code is sustained by the spectral supplement of the Name of the Father, the obscene spectre of the Freudian "primordial father."[14] Therein, too, resides the lesson of Coppola's *Apocalypse Now*: in the figure of Kurtz, the Freudian "primordial father"–the obscene father whose enjoyment is subordinate to no symbolic law, the total Master who dares to confront face-to-face the Real of terrifying enjoyment–is presented not as a remainder of some barbaric past, but as the necessary outcome of modern Western power itself. Kurtz was a perfect soldier. Through his over-identification with the military power system, he turned into the excessive figure the system has to eliminate. The ultimate horizon of *Apocalypse Now* is this insight into how power generates its own excess which it has to annihilate in an operation which has to imitate what it fights. Willard's mission to kill Kurtz does not appear on the official record: "It never happened," as the general who briefs Willard points out. We have entered the domain of secret operations, of what power does without ever admitting it. This is where Christopher Hitchens missed the point when he wrote of the Abu Ghraib jailers:

> One of two things must necessarily be true. Either these goons were acting on someone's authority, in which case there is a layer of mid- to high-level people who think that they are not bound by the laws and codes and standing orders. Or they were acting on their own authority, in which case they are the equivalent of mutineers, deserters, or traitors in the field. This is why one asks wistfully if there is no provision in the

procedures of military justice for them to be taken out and shot.[15]

The problem is that the Abu Ghraib tortures were *neither* of these two options: while they cannot be reduced to simple evil acts of individual soldiers, they were, of course, also not directly ordered–they were legitimised by a specific version of the obscene Code Red. To claim that they were the acts of "mutineers, deserters, or traitors in the field" is the same nonsense as the claim that the Ku Klux Klan lynchings were the acts of traitors to Western Christian civilisation and not the outburst of its own obscene underside; or that acts of child abuse by Catholic priests are perpetrated by "traitors" to Catholicism ... Abu Ghraib was not simply a case of American arrogance towards a Third World people: in being submitted to humiliating tortures, the Iraqi prisoners were effectively *initiated into American culture.* They were given a taste of its obscene underside, which forms the necessary supplement to the public values of personal dignity, democracy, and freedom. Bush was thus wrong: what we are getting when we see the photos of the humiliated Iraqi prisoners on our screens and front pages is precisely a direct insight into American values, into the very core of the obscene enjoyment that sustains the U.S. way of life. These photos put into an adequate perspective Samuel Huntington's well-known thesis on the ongoing "clash of civilisations." The clash between the Arab and American civilisations is not a clash between barbarism and respect for human dignity, but a clash between anonymous brutal torture and torture as a media spectacle in which the victims' bodies serve as the anonymous background for the grinning "innocent American" faces of the torturers themselves. It seems, to paraphrase Walter Benjamin, that every clash of civilisations really is a clash of underlying barbarisms.

6

Allegro

DIVINE VIOLENCE

Benjamin with Hitchcock

In Alfred Hitchcock's film *Psycho,* the staircase murder of the detective Arbogast gives us the Hitchcockian God's-point-of-view shot. We see the entire scene of the first-floor corridor and stairs from above. When the shrieking creature enters the frame and starts to stab Arbogast, we pass to the creature's subjective point of view, a close-up of Arbogast's face falling down the stairs and being sliced up–as if, in this twist from an objective to a subjective shot, God himself has lost his neutrality and "fallen into" the world, brutally intervening, delivering justice.[1] "Divine violence" stands for such brutal intrusions of justice beyond law.

In the ninth of his "Theses on the Philosophy of History," Walter Benjamin refers to Paul Klee's painting *Angelus Novus,* which

> shows an angel looking as though he is about to move away from something he is fixedly contemplating. His eyes are staring, his mouth is open, his wings are spread. This is how one pictures the angel of history. His face is turned toward the past. Where we perceive a chain of events, he sees one single catastrophe which keeps piling wreckage and hurls it in front of his feet. The angel would like to stay, awaken the dead, and make whole what has been smashed. But a storm is blowing in

from Paradise; it has got caught in his wings with such a violence that the angel can no longer close them. The storm irresistibly propels him into the future to which his back is turned, while the pile of debris before him grows skyward. This storm is what we call progress.[2]

And what if divine violence is the wild intervention of this angel? Seeing the pile of debris which grows skyward, this wreckage of injustices, from time to time he strikes back to restore the balance, to enact a revenge for the destructive impact of "progress." Couldn't the entire history of humanity be seen as a growing normalisation of injustice, entailing the nameless and faceless suffering of millions? Somewhere, in the sphere of the "divine," perhaps these injustices are not forgotten. They are accumulated, the wrongs are registered, the tension grows more and more unbearable, till divine violence explodes in a retaliatory destructive rage.[3]

Opposite such a violent enforcement of justice stands the figure of divine violence as unjust, as an explosion of divine caprice whose exemplary case is, of course, that of Job. After Job is hit by calamities, his theological friends come, offering interpretations which render these calamities meaningful. The greatness of Job is not so much to protest his innocence as to insist on the meaninglessness of his calamities. When God finally appears, he affirms Job's position against the theological defenders of the faith.

The structure here is exactly the same as that of Freud's dream of Irma's injection, which begins with a conversation between Freud and his patient Irma about the failure of her treatment owing to an infected injection.

In the course of the conversation, Freud gets closer to her, approaches her face, and looks deep into her mouth, confronting the dreadful sight of her live red flesh. At the point of unbearable horror, the tonality of the dream changes and terror abruptly passes into comedy: three doctors appear, Freud's friends, who in ridiculous pseudo-professional jargon enumerate multiple– and mutually exclusive–reasons why Irma's poisoning by the infected injection was nobody's fault: there was no injection, the injection was untainted ... So first there is a traumatic encounter, the sight of the raw flesh of Irma's throat, followed by the sudden leap into comedy, into the exchange between three ridiculous doctors which enables the dreamer to avoid the encounter of the true trauma. The function of the three doctors is the same as that of the three theological friends in the story of Job: to disguise the impact of the trauma with a symbolic semblance.

This resistance to meaning is crucial when we are confronting potential or actual catastrophes, from AIDS and ecological disaster to the Holocaust: they refuse "deeper meaning." This legacy of Job prevents us from taking refuge in the standard transcendent figure of God as a secret Master who knows the meaning of what appears to us as meaningless catastrophe, the God who sees the entire picture in which what we perceive as a stain contributes to global harmony. When confronted with an event like the Holocaust or the death of millions in the Congo over these last years, is it not obscene to claim that these stains have a deeper meaning through which they contribute to the harmony of the whole? Is there a whole which can teleologically justify and thus redeem or sublate an event such as the Holocaust? Christ's death on the cross surely means one should unreservedly drop the notion of God as a transcendent caretaker who guarantees the happy outcome of our acts, i.e., who enforces historical teleology. Christ's death on the cross is in itself the death of this *protecting* God. It is a repetition of Job's stance: it refuses any "deeper meaning" that might cover up the brutal reality of historical catastrophes.[4]

There is a Hitchcockian resonance to the iconography of the 9/11 catastrophe: the endlessly repeated shot of the plane approaching and hitting the second World Trade Center tower erupts like a real-life version of the famous scene from *The Birds* in which Melanie advances toward the Bodega Bay pier in her small boat. While approaching the wharf, she waves to her (future) lover. A single bird, first perceived as an undistinguishable dark blot, unexpectedly enters the frame from above right and hits her head.[5] The plane which hit the World Trade Center tower could literally be understood as the ultimate Hitchcockian blot, the anamorphic stain which denaturalised the idyllic New York landscape. The attacking birds are the last element in the triad of *North by Northwest, Psycho,* and *The Birds*: first, the plane, a metaphor for a bird, attacks the hero in the famous sequence on the prairie plains outside Chicago; then, Norman Bates's room is full of stuffed birds (a metonymy); finally, birds themselves attack.

Two Hollywood productions were released to mark the fifth anniversary of 9/11: Paul Greengrass's *United 93* and Oliver Stone's *World Trade Center*. The first thing that strikes the eye about these films is that both try to be as anti-Hollywood as possible. They focus on the courage of ordinary people, with no glamorous stars, no special effects, no grandiloquent heroic gestures, just a terse realistic depiction of everyday people in extraordinary circumstances. However, both films also contain notable formal exceptions: moments which violate their basic style. *United* 93 starts with kidnappers in a motel room, praying, getting ready. They look austere, like angels of death of some kind. The first shot after the title credits confirms this impression: it is a panoramic view from high above Manhattan at night, accompanied by the sound of the kidnappers' prayers, as if the kidnappers are floating above the city preparing to descend on earth to reap their harvest. Similarly, there are no direct shots of the planes hitting the towers in *World Trade Center*. All that we see, seconds before the catastrophe, is a policeman on a busy street in a crowd of people and an ominous shadow quickly passing over them–the shadow of the first plane. (Significantly, after the policemen-heroes are caught in the rubble, the camera, in a Hitchcockian move, withdraws back into the air to a "God's view" of New York City.) This direct passage from down-to-earth daily life to the view from above confers on both films a strange theological reverberation–as if the "terrorist" attacks were a kind of divine intervention. What can this mean?

The first reaction of right-wing Christians Jerry Falwell and Pat Robertson to the 9/11 bombings was to see them as a sign that God had lifted his protection from the United States because of the sinful lives of Americans. They blamed hedonist materialism, liberalism, and rampant sexuality, and claimed that America had

got what it deserved. The fact that the very same condemnation of liberal America voiced by the Muslim
Other also came from the heart of *l'Amérique profonde*
should give us pause for reflection.

In an oblique way, *United* 93 and *World Trade Center*
tend to the opposite interpretation: they want to read
the 9/11 catastrophe as a blessing in disguise, as a divine
intervention which has served to waken America from
its moral slumber and to bring out the best in its people.
WTC ends with the off-screen words which spell out
its message: terrible events, like the destruction of the
Twin Towers, bring out the worst AND the best in
people–courage, solidarity, sacrifice for the community.
People are shown able to do things they never imagined. This utopian perspective is one of the undercur-
rents that sustain our fascination with disaster movies:
it is as if our societies need a major catastrophe in order
to resuscitate the spirit of communal solidarity.

Against all such temptations to seek a "deeper meaning," G. K. Chesterton is right when he concludes "The
Oracle of the Dog" with Father Brown's defence of com-
monsense reality in which things are just what they are,
not bearers of hidden mystical meanings, and of the
Christian miracle of incarnation as the exception that
guarantees and sustains common reality:

> "People readily swallow the untested claims of this, that,
> or the other. It's drowning all your old rationalism and
> scepticism, it's coming in like a sea; and the name of it is
> superstition." He stood up abruptly, his face heavy with
> a sort of frown, and went on talking almost as if he were
> alone. "It's the first effect of not believing in God that

you lose your common sense and can't see things as
they are. Anything that anybody talks about, and says
there's a good deal in it, extends itself indefinitely like a
vista in a nightmare. And a dog is an omen, and a cat is
a mystery, and a pig is a mascot, and a beetle is a scarab,
calling up all the menagerie of polytheism from Egypt
and old India; Dog Anubis and great green-eyed Pasht
and all the holy howling Bulls of Bashan; reeling back to
the bestial gods of the beginning, escaping into
elephants and snakes and crocodiles; and all because
you are frightened of four words:
"He was made Man."[6]

It was thus his very Christianity that made Chesterton
prefer prosaic explanations to the all-too-fast resort to
supernatural magic. This is where his engagement with
detective fiction begins: if a jewel is stolen from a locked
container, the solution is not telekinesis but the use of a
strong magnet or some other sleight of hand; if a person
vanishes unexpectedly, there must be a secret tunnel.
Naturalistic explanations are *more* magic than a resort
to supernatural intervention. The detective's explanation of a tricky deceit by means of which the criminal
accomplished the murder in a locked room is far more
"magical" than the claim that he possessed the supernatural ability to move through walls!

One is tempted to go even a step further here and
give Chesterton's last lines a different reading—no doubt
not intended by Chesterton, but none the less closer to a
weird truth. When people imagine all kinds of deeper
meanings because they "are frightened of four words:
'He was made Man,'" what really frightens them is that

they will lose their transcendent God. This is the God who guarantees the meaning of the universe, the God who is a hidden master pulling all strings. Instead, Chesterton gives us a God who abandons this transcendent position and throws himself into his own creation. This man-God fully engages with the world, even dies. We humans are left with no higher power watching over us, only the terrible burden of freedom and responsibility for the fate of divine creation, and thus for God himself.

Divine Violence: What It Is Not . . .

Our first conclusion must be that Benjamin's understanding of "divine violence" had nothing to do with the terrorist violence executed by today's religious fundamentalists who pretend they are acting on behalf of God and as instruments of the Divine Will–even though media coverage would induce us to leap to such an association. The most obvious candidate for "divine violence" is the violent explosion of resentment which finds expression in a spectrum that ranges from mob lynchings to organised revolutionary terror. One of the main tasks of today's "post-left" is to refer to this area of violence in order to denounce the very idea of revolution. The latest representative of this tendency is the German philosopher Peter Sloterdijk, whose standard procedure is to supplement a well-known philosophical category with its neglected opposite. Say, in his critical reading of Heidegger, he adds to the Heideggerian "being-towards-death" the opposite trauma of birth, of being born into, thrown into, the opening of life.[7] In a similar way, his *Rage and Time* (*Zorn und Zeit,* an allusion to

Heidegger's *Sein und Zeit*) supplements the predominant erotic logic with its neglected counterpart, *thymos*. *Eros* (the possession of objects, their production and enjoyment) is set up against *thymos* (envy, competition, recognition).[8]

Sloterdijk's premise is that one can grasp the true meaning of the events of 1990, focused on the disintegration of communist regimes, only against the background of *thymos*. That year signalled both the end of state revolutionary emancipatory logic and the end of the entire Messianic logic of rage-concentration and total revenge that exploded with Judeo-Christianity and whose secularisation was the communist project. Sloterdijk thus proposes an alternative history of the West as the history of *rage*. The *Iliad*, the founding text of the West, begins with the word "rage": Homer appeals to the goddess to help him sing the song of the rage of Achilles and its dire consequences. Although the dispute between Achilles and Agamemnon concerns the erotic—Agamemnon took the slave Briseis from Achilles—Briseis is not an object of intense erotic investment, but in herself totally irrelevant. What matters is not frustrated sexual gratification, but hurt pride. What is crucial, however, in this position is the later monotheistic, Judeo-Christian mutation of rage. While in ancient Greece rage is allowed to explode directly, what follows is its sublimation, temporal deferral, postponement, transference: not we, but God, should keep the books of wrongs and settle accounts in the Last Judgment. The Christian prohibition of revenge ("turn the other cheek") is strictly a correlative to the apocalyptic scenery of the Last Days.

This idea of Judgment Day, when all accumulated debts will be fully paid and an out-of-joint world will finally be set straight, is then taken over in secularised form by the modern leftist project. Here the agent of judgment is no longer God, but the people. Leftist political movements are like "banks of rage." They collect rage investments from people and promise them large-scale revenge, the re-establishment of global justice. Since, after the revolutionary explosion of rage, full satisfaction never takes place and an inequality and hierarchy re-emerge, there always arises a push for the *second*–true, integral–revolution which will satisfy the disappointed and truly finish the emancipatory work: 1792 after 1789, October after February . . .

The problem is simply that there is never enough rage capital. This is why it is necessary to borrow from or combine with other rages: national or cultural. In fascism, the national rage predominates; Mao's communism mobilises the rage of exploited poor farmers, not proletarians. No wonder that Sloterdijk systematically uses the term "leftist fascism," and regularly refers to Ernst Nolte, the German "revisionist" historian who developed the idea of Nazism as a deplorable but understandable reaction to communist terror. For Sloterdijk, fascism is ultimately a secondary variation of (and reaction to) the properly leftist project of emancipatory rage. In our own time, when this global rage has exhausted its potential, two main forms of rage remain: Islam (the rage of the victims of capitalist globalisation) plus "irrational" outbursts by youth. One should, perhaps, add to these Latin-American populism, ecologists, anti-consumerists, and other forms of anti-globalist resentment. The Porto Alegre movement failed to establish itself as a global bank for this rage, since it lacked a positive alternative vision. Sloterdijk even mentions the "re-emerging Left-Fascist whispering at the borders of academia,"[9] where, I guess, I belong . . . Although these local outbursts are what critics of Fukuyama celebrate as the "return of history," they remain poor substitutes which cannot hide the fact that there is no longer a global rage potential.

So what is Sloterdijk's programme? One needs to move "Beyond Resentment," as the title of the book's last sub-chapter would have it. One needs to de-legitimate the fatal link between intellectuals and resentment in all its forms, including the respectful feminist, post-colonialist, and ecological ones. One should reassert the liberal approach whose first formulation was John Locke's triad life–freedom–property, cured by the Nietzschean bitter anti-resentment pill. We need to learn to live in a post-monotheist world culture, in an anti-authoritarian meritocracy which respects civilised norms and personal rights, in a balance between elitism and egalitarianism. We need to articulate a liberal "code of conduct" that succeeds in balancing the interplay of multiple thymotic agents, and thus prevents the fatal flow towards ecological and ethical destruction. No wonder that Sloterdijk is closely linked with the French philosopher Alain Finkielkraut, with whom he published a book of dialogues: though in a different ideological context, Finkielkraut fights along the same anti-"totalitarian" lines. So, back to Benjamin, does his conception of divine violence also point towards explosions of resentment? We need a double strategy here; to begin with we need to rehabilitate the notion of resentment. Recall what W. G. Sebald wrote about Jean Améry's confrontation with the trauma of the Nazi concentration camps:

> The energy behind Améry's polemics derived from implacable resentment. A large number of his essays are concerned with justifying this emotion (commonly regarded as a warped need for revenge) as essential to a truly critical view of the past. Resentment, writes Améry in full awareness of the illogicality of his attempt at a definition, "nails every one of us unto the cross of his ruined past. Absurdly, it demands that the irreversible be turned around, that the event be undone."[...] The issue, then, is not to resolve but to reveal the conflict. The spur of resentment which Améry conveys to us in his polemic demands recognition of the *right* to resentment, entailing no less than a programmatic attempt to sensitize the consciousness of a people "already rehabilitated by time."[10]

When a subject is hurt in such a devastating way that the very idea of revenge according to *ius talionis* is no less ridiculous than the promise of the reconciliation with the perpetrator after the perpetrator's atonement, the only thing that remains is to persist in the "unremitting denunciation of injustice." One should give this stance its full anti-Nietzschean weight: here, resentment has nothing to do with the slave morality. It stands rather for a refusal to "normalise" the crime, to make it part of the ordinary/explicable/accountable flow of things, to integrate it into a consistent and meaningful life-narrative; after all possible explanations, it returns with its question: "Yes, I got all this, but nevertheless, *how could you have done it*? Your story about it doesn't make sense!" In other words, the resentment for which Sebald pleads is a Nietzschean heroic resentment, a refusal to compromise, an insistence "against all odds."

How, then, does this authentic resentment relate to the triad of punishment (revenge), forgiveness, and forgetting, as the three standard ways of dealing with a crime? The first thing to do here is to assert the priority of the Jewish principle of just revenge/punishment–an "eye for an eye," the *ius talionis*–over the standard formula of "we will forgive your crime, but we will not forget it." The only way truly to forgive *and* forget is to enact a revenge (or a just punishment): after the criminal is properly punished, I can move forward and leave the whole affair behind. There is thus something liberating in being properly punished for one's crime: I paid my debt to society and I am free again, no past burdens attached. The "merciful" logic of "forgive, but not forget" is, on the contrary, much more oppressive: I (the criminal who is forgiven) remain forever haunted by the crime I committed, since the crime was not "undone (*ungeschehengemacht*)," retroactively cancelled, erased, in what Hegel sees as the meaning of punishment.

Rigorous Jewish justice and Christian mercy, the inexplicable gesture of undeserved pardon, stand opposed. In the Christian view, we humans were born in sin. We cannot ever repay our debts and redeem ourselves through our own acts. Our only salvation lies in God's mercy, in his supreme sacrifice. Yet in this very gesture of breaking the chain of justice through the

inexplicable act of mercy, of paying our debt, Christianity imposes on us an even stronger debt: we are forever
indebted to Christ, we cannot ever repay him for what
he did for us. The Freudian name for such excessive
pressure which we cannot ever remunerate is, of course,
superego. Usually, it is Judaism which is conceived as
the religion of the superego and of man's subordination
to a jealous, mighty, and severe God, in contrast to the
God of mercy and love who is Christian. However, it is
precisely through *not* demanding from us the price for
our sins, through paying this price for us himself, that
the Christian God of mercy establishes himself as the
supreme superego agency: "I paid the highest price
for your sins, and you are thus indebted to me *for
ever* . . ."[11]

In a letter to his father, Franz Kafka notes this same
paradox of mercy (grace): "from the many occasions on
which I had, according to your clearly expressed opinion, deserved a beating but was let off at the last moment by your grace, I again accumulated only a huge
sense of guilt. On every side I was to blame, I was in
your debt."[12] The contours of this God as the superego
agency whose very mercy generates the indelible guilt of
believers are discernible up to Stalin. One should never
forget that, as the now available minutes of the meetings
of the Politburo and Central Committee from the 1930s
demonstrate, Stalin's direct interventions were as a rule
ones which displayed mercy. When younger CC members, eager to prove their revolutionary fervour, demanded an instant death penalty for Bukharin, Stalin
always intervened and said, "Patience! His guilt is not
yet proven!" or something similar. Of course this was a

hypocritical attitude–Stalin was well aware that he himself generated the destructive fervour, that the younger members were eager to please him–but none the less, the appearance of mercy is necessary here.

There is thus more than tasteless irony in proposing a pseudo-dialectical synthesis of the two terms as a way of resolving the eternal dilemma "to punish or to forgive": first, punish the perpetrator, then forgive him . . . Is this not the final outcome of Lars von Trier's "feminine" trilogy of *Breaking the Waves*, *Dancer in the Dark*, and *Dogville*? In all three films, the heroine (Emily Watson, Björk, Nicole Kidman) is exposed to terrifying, if not outrageously melodramatic, suffering and humiliation; however, while in the first two films the heroine's ordeal culminates in a painfully desperate death, in *Dogville* she mercilessly strikes back and exacts full revenge for the despicable way the residents of the small town where she took refuge treated her, personally killing her ex-lover. ("There are some things you have to do yourself.") This denouement cannot but give rise, in the spectator, to a deep if ethically problematic satisfaction–all the wrongdoers certainly receive their comeuppance with interest. We could also give all this a feminist twist: after the spectacle of feminine masochist suffering dragged on to an unbearable length, the victim finally gathers the strength to strike back with a vengeance, asserting herself as a subject regaining full control over her predicament. We thus seem to get the best of both worlds: our thirst for vengeance is not only satisfied, but even legitimised in feminist terms. What spoils this easy solution is not the predictable (but false) feminist counter-argument that her victory is paid for by her adopting a "masculine" violent attitude. There is another feature which should be given its full weight: the heroine of *Dogville* is only able to enact her ruthless revenge the moment her father (a mafia boss) comes to the city in search of her. In short, her active role signals her renewed submission under paternal authority.

Another approach to the trilogy would be to read *Dogville* as, quite literally, the film of true mercy. Grace lacks mercy insofar as she patronisingly "understands" the inhabitants, offering them her services, silently enduring her ordeal, refusing revenge. Her gangster father is right: *this* is her arrogance. It is only when she decides on her revenge that she effectively acts as and becomes one of them, losing her arrogant, superior position. In killing them, she recognises them in a Hegelian way. When she sees them in a "new light," she sees them as they are, not the idealised poor, small town people. Her act of killing is thus an act of true mercy.

The big argument of anti-(death-)penalty advocates is the arrogance of punishing other human beings, or even killing them. What gives us the right to do this? Are we really in a position to judge? The best answer to this is to turn the argument round. What is really arrogant and sinful is to assume the prerogative of mercy. Who among us, ordinary mortals, especially if we are not the culprit's immediate victim, has the right to erase another's crime, to treat it with leniency? Only God himself–or in state terms, the very pinnacle of power, king or president–has, owing to his exceptional position, the prerogative of erasing another's guilt. Our duty is to act according to the logic of justice and punish crime: *not* to do so entails the true blasphemy of elevating oneself to the level of God, of acting with his authority.

How, then, does authentic resentment come into all this? As the supplementary fourth term in the triad of punishment (revenge), forgiveness, and forgetting, it enters the stage as the only authentic stance when we are dealing with a crime of such monstrosity–like the killing of European Jews by the Nazis–that all the first three stances lose their impact. One cannot forgive, even less forget, such an act, no more than one can adequately punish it.

This brings us back to Sloterdijk: wherefrom Sloterdijk's denouncing of every global emancipatory project as a case of envy and resentment? Wherefrom his obsessive-compulsive urge to find beneath solidarity the envy of the weak and their thirst for revenge? In short, wherefrom his unbound "hermeneutics of suspicion" *à la* caricaturised Nietzsche? What if *this very urge is sustained by a disavowed envy and resentment of its own, the envy of the universal emancipatory position,* which is why one HAS to find some dirt in its foundation which would deprive it of its purity?[13] The object of envy is here the MIRACLE of ethical universality which cannot be reduced to a distorted effect of "lower" libidinal processes.

Perhaps the key achievement of Jacques Lacan's reading of *Antigone* is to insist on this point: we find in it no expected "Freudian" themes, nothing about the incestuous link of brother and sister.[14] Therein resides also the point of Lacan's "Kant with Sade."[15] Today, in our post-idealist era of the "hermeneutics of suspicion," doesn't everybody know what the point of the "with" is—the truth of Kant's ethical rigorism is the sadism of the law, i.e., the Kantian law is a superego agency that sadistically enjoys the subject's deadlock, his inability to meet its inexorable demands, like the proverbial teacher who tortures pupils with impossible tasks and secretly savours their failings? Lacan's point, however, is the exact opposite of this first association: it is not Kant who was a closet sadist, it is Sade who was a closet Kantian. That is to say, what one should bear in mind is that the focus of Lacan is always Kant, not Sade: what he is interested in are the ultimate consequences and disavowed premises of the Kantian ethical revolution. In other words, Lacan does not try to make the usual "reductionist" point that every ethical act, as pure and disinterested as it may appear, is always grounded in some "pathological" motivation (the agent's own long-term interest, the admiration of his peers, up to the "negative" satisfaction provided by the suffering and extortion often demanded by ethical acts). The focus of Lacan's interest rather resides in the paradoxical reversal by means of which desire itself (i.e., acting upon one's desire, not compromising it) can no longer be grounded in any "pathological" interest or motivation, and thus meets the criteria of the Kantian ethical act, so that "following one's desire" overlaps with "doing one's duty." This is why Lacan, in his notion of the act, reverses the standard "hermeneutics of suspicion": when Kant himself, driven by suspicion, admits that we cannot ever be sure if what we did was truly an ethical act and not secretly sustained by some "pathological" motif (even if this motif is the narcissistic satisfaction brought about by the fact that we did

our duty), he commits an error. What is truly traumatic for the subject is not the fact that a pure ethical
act is (perhaps) impossible, that freedom is (perhaps)
an appearance, based on our ignorance of the true
motivations of our acts; what is truly traumatic is freedom itself, the fact that freedom IS possible, and we
desperately search for some "pathological" determina-
tions in order to avoid this fact. In other words, true
Freudian theory has nothing to do with reducing ethical autonomy to an illusion based on repressing our
"low" libidinal motifs.

. . . And Finally, What It Is!

Interpreters of Benjamin struggle with what "divine violence" might actually mean. Is it yet another leftist
dream of a "pure" event which never really takes place?
One should recall here Friedrich Engels's 1891 reference
to the Paris Commune as an example of the dictatorship of the proletariat:

> Of late, the Social-Democratic philistine has once more
> been filled with wholesome terror at the words:
> Dictatorship of the Proletariat. Well and good,
> gentlemen, do you want to know what this dictatorship
> looks like? Look at the Paris Commune. That was the
> Dictatorship of the Proletariat.[16]

One could repeat this, *mutatis mutandis*, apropos divine violence: "Well and good, gentlemen critical theorists, do you want to know what this divine violence
looks like? Look at the revolutionary Terror of 1792–94.
That was the Divine Violence." (And the series could go
on: the Red Terror of 1919 . . .) That is to say, perhaps we

should fearlessly identify divine violence with positively existing historical phenomena, thus avoiding any obscurantist mystification.

Here are some passages from the dense last pages of Benjamin's "Critique of Violence":

Just as in all spheres God opposes myth, mythic violence is confronted by the divine. And the latter constitutes its antithesis in all respects. If mythic violence is law-making, divine violence is law-destroying; if the former sets boundaries, the latter boundlessly destroys them; if mythic violence brings at once guilt and retribution, divine power only expiates; if the former threatens, the latter strikes; if the former is bloody, the latter is lethal without spilling blood. [. . .] For blood is the symbol of mere life. The dissolution of legal violence stems [. . .] from the guilt of mere natural life, which consigns the living, innocent and unhappy, to a retribution that "expiates" the guilt of mere life–and doubtless also purifies the guilty, not of guilt, however, but of law. For with mere life, the rule of law over the living ceases. Mythical violence is bloody power over mere life for its own sake, divine violence is pure power over all life for the sake of the living. The first demands sacrifice; the second accepts it.

[. . .] the question "May I kill?" meets its irreducible answer in the commandment "Thou shalt not kill." This commandment precedes the deed, just as God was "preventing" the deed. But just as it may not be fear of punishment that enforces obedience, the injunction becomes inapplicable, incommensurable, once the deed is accomplished. No judgment of the

deed can be derived from the commandment. And so
neither the divine judgment nor the grounds for this
judgment can be known in advance. Those who base
a condemnation of all violent killing of one person by
another on the commandment are therefore mistaken.
It exists not as a criterion of judgment, but as a
guideline for the actions of persons or communities
who have to wrestle with it in solitude and, in
exceptional cases, to take upon themselves the
responsibility of ignoring it.[17]

It is this domain of pure divine violence which is the
domain of sovereignty, the domain within which killing
is neither an expression of personal pathology (idiosyncratic, destructive drive), nor a crime (or its punishment), nor a sacred sacrifice. It is neither aesthetic, nor
ethical, nor religious (a sacrifice to dark gods). So, paradoxically, divine violence does partially overlap with
the bio-political disposal of *Homini sacer*: in both cases,
killing is neither a crime nor a sacrifice. Those annihi-
lated by divine violence are fully and completely guilty:
they are not sacrificed, since they are not worthy of being sacrificed to and accepted by God–they are annihi-
lated without being made a sacrifice. Of what are they
guilty? Of leading a mere (natural) life. Divine violence
purifies the guilty not of guilt but of law, because law is
limited to the living: it cannot reach beyond life to touch
what is in excess of life, what is more than mere life.
Divine violence is an expression of pure drive, of the
undeadness, the excess of life, which strikes at "bare
life" regulated by law. The "theological" dimension without which, for Benjamin, revolution cannot win is the

very dimension of the excess of drive, of its "too-muchness."[18]

It is mythical violence that demands sacrifice, and holds power over bare life; whereas divine violence is non-sacrificial and expiatory. One should therefore not be afraid to assert the formal parallel between the state annihilation of *Homini sacer,* for example the Nazi killing of the Jews, and the revolutionary terror, where one can also kill without committing a crime and without sacrifice—the difference resides in the fact that the Nazi killing remains a means of the state power. While, in the concluding paragraph, Benjamin asserts that "revolutionary violence, the highest manifestation of unalloyed violence by man, is possible," he adds a key qualification:

> Less possible and also less urgent for humankind,
> however, is to decide when unalloyed violence has been
> realized in particular cases. For only mythic violence,
> not divine, will be recognizable as such with certainty,
> unless it be in incomparable effects, because the
> expiatory power of violence is invisible to men. [. . .]
> Divine violence may manifest itself in a true war as it
> does in the crowd's divine judgment on a criminal. [. . .]
> Divine violence, which is the sign and seal but never the
> means of sacred dispatch, may be called "sovereign"
> violence.[19]

It is crucial to interpret the last sentence correctly: the opposition of mythic and divine violence is that between the means and the sign, that is, mythic violence is a means to establish the rule of Law (the legal social order), while divine violence serves no means, not even that of punishing the culprits and thus re-establishing the equilibrium of justice. It is just the sign of the injustice of the world, of the world being ethically "out of joint." This, however, does *not* imply that divine justice has a meaning: rather, it is a sign without meaning, and the temptation to be resisted is precisely the one which Job resisted successfully, the temptation to provide it with some "deeper meaning." What this entails is that, to put it in Badiou's terms, mythic violence belongs to the order of Being, while divine violence belongs to the order of Event: there are no "objective" criteria enabling us to identify an act of violence as divine; the same act that, to an external observer, is merely an outburst of violence can be divine for those engaged in it–there is no big Other guaranteeing its divine nature; the risk of reading and assuming it as divine is fully the subject's own. It is like what Jansenism teaches about miracles: miracles cannot be verified objectively; for a neutral observer, they can always be accounted for in the terms of ordinary natural causality. It is only for the believer that an event is a miracle.

When Benjamin writes that the prohibition on killing is "a guideline for the actions of persons or communities who have to wrestle with it in solitude and, in exceptional cases, to take upon themselves the responsibility of ignoring it," does he not propose to read it as a Kantian regulative Idea, not a direct constitutive principle of ethical reality? Note how Benjamin opposes here the "totalitarian" justification of killing done by those who act as instruments of the big Other (historical necessity, etc.): one has to "wrestle with it in solitude," assuming full responsibility for it. In other words, "divine violence" has nothing to do with outbursts of "sacred madness," with that bacchanalia in which subjects resign their autonomy and responsibility since it is some larger divine power which acts through them.

Divine violence is precisely not a direct intervention of an omnipotent God to punish humankind for its excesses, a kind of preview or foretaste of the Last Judgment: the ultimate distinction between divine violence and the impotent/violent *passages a l'acte* of us, humans, is that, far from expressing divine omnipotence, divine violence is *a sign of God's (the big Other's) own impotence.* All that changes between divine violence and a blind *passage a l'acte* is the *site* of impotence.

Divine violence is not the repressed illegal origin of the legal order—the Jacobin revolutionary Terror is not the "dark origin" of the bourgeois order, in the sense of the heroic-criminal state-founding violence celebrated by Heidegger. Divine violence is thus to be distinguished from state sovereignty as the exception which founds the law, as well as from pure violence as anarchic explosion. With regard to the French Revolution, it was, significantly, Danton, *not* Robespierre, who provided the most concise formula of the imperceptible shift from "dictatorship of the proletariat" to statist violence, or in Benjamin's terms, from divine to mythic violence: "Let us be terrible so that the people will not have to be."[20] For Danton, the Jacobin, revolutionary state terror was a kind of pre-emptive action whose true aim was not revenge on the enemies but to prevent the direct "divine" violence of the *sans-culottes,* of the people themselves. In other words, let us do what the people demand of us *so that they will not do it themselves* . . .

Divine violence should thus be conceived as divine in the precise sense of the old Latin motto *vox populi, vox dei: not* in the perverse sense of "we are doing it as mere instruments of the People's Will," but as the heroic assumption of the solitude of sovereign decision. It is a decision (to kill, to risk or lose one's own life) made in absolute solitude, with no cover in the big Other. If it is extra-moral, it is not "immoral," it does not give the agent licence just to kill with some kind of angelic innocence. When those outside the structured social field strike "blindly," demanding and enacting immediate justice/vengeance, this is divine violence. Recall, a decade or so ago, the panic in Rio de Janeiro when crowds descended from the favelas into the rich part of the city and started looting and burning supermarkets. This was indeed divine violence . . . They were like biblical locusts, the divine punishment for men's sinful ways. This divine violence strikes out of nowhere, a means without end–or, as Robespierre put it in his speech in which he demanded the execution of Louis XVI:

> Peoples do not judge in the same way as courts of law; they do not hand down sentences, they throw thunderbolts; they do not condemn kings, they drop them back into the void; and this justice is worth just as much as that of the courts.[21]

This is why, as was clear to Robespierre, without the "faith" in (a purely axiomatic presupposition of) the eternal idea of freedom which persists through all defeats, a revolution "is just a noisy crime that destroys another crime." This faith is most poignantly expressed in Robespierre's very last speech on 8 Thermidor 1794, the day before his arrest and execution:

> But there do exist, I can assure you, souls that are feeling and pure; it exists, that tender, imperious and irresistible passion, the torment and delight of magnanimous hearts; that deep horror of tyranny, that compassionate zeal for the oppressed, that sacred love for the homeland, that even more sublime and holy love for humanity, without which a great revolution is just a noisy crime that destroys another crime; it does exist, that generous ambition to establish here on earth the world's first Republic.[22]

The implication of these lines is, again, that divine violence belongs to the order of Event: as such, its status is radically subjective, it is the subject's *work of love*. Two (in)famous passages from Che Guevara bring this point home:

> At the risk of seeming ridiculous, let me say that the true revolutionary is guided by a great feeling of love. It is impossible to think of a genuine revolutionary lacking this quality.[23]

> Hatred is an element of struggle; relentless hatred of the enemy that impels us over and beyond the natural limitations of man and transforms us into effective, violent, selective, and cold killing machines. Our soldiers must be thus; a people without hatred cannot vanquish a brutal enemy.[24]

These two apparently opposite stances are united in Che's motto: *"Hay que endurecerse sin perder jamás la ternura."* (One must endure–become hard, toughen oneself–without losing tenderness.)[25] Or to paraphrase Kant and Robespierre yet again: love without cruelty is powerless; cruelty without love is blind, a short-lived passion which loses its persistent edge. The underlying paradox is that what makes love angelic, what elevates it over mere unstable and pathetic sentimentality, is its cruelty itself, its link with violence–it is this link which raises it "over and beyond the natural limitations of man" and thus transforms it into an unconditional drive. So while Che Guevara certainly believed in the transformative power of love, he would never have been heard humming "love is all you need"–you need to *love with hatred*. Or as Kierkegaard put it long ago: the necessary consequence (the "truth") of the Christian demand to *love one's enemy* is

> the demand to *hate the beloved* out of love and in love . . . So high–humanly speaking to a kind of madness–can Christianity press the demand of love if love is to be the fulfilling of the law. Therefore it teaches that the Christian shall, if it is demanded, be capable of hating his father and mother and sister and beloved.[26]

Kierkegaard applies here the logic of *hainamoration*, later articulated by Lacan, which relies on the split in the beloved between the beloved person and the true object-cause of my love for him, that which is "in him more than himself" (for Kierkegaard: God). Sometimes, hatred is the only proof that I really love you.

The notion of love should be given here all its Paulinian weight: *the domain of pure violence,* the domain outside law (legal power), the domain of the violence which is neither law-founding nor law-sustaining, *is the domain of love.*

Epilogue

ADAGIO

The circle of our investigation is thus closed: we have travelled from the rejection of false anti-violence to the endorsement of emancipatory violence. We started with the hypocrisy of those who, while combating *subjective violence,* commit *systemic violence* that generates the very phenomena they abhor. We located the ultimate cause of violence in the *fear of the Neighbour,* and showed how it is founded in the *violence that inheres to language itself,* the very medium of overcoming direct violence. We went on to analyse three types of violence which haunt our media: the "irrational" *youth outbursts* in Paris suburbs in 2005, the recent *terrorist attacks,* the *chaos in New Orleans* after hurricane Katrina. We then went on to demonstrate the *antinomies of tolerant reason* apropos the violent demonstrations against the caricatures of Muhammad in a Danish newspaper. We deployed the limitation of *tolerance* as the predominant notion underpinning today's ideology. Finally, we tackled directly the emancipatory dimension of the category of *divine violence,* as it was articulated by Walter Benjamin. What, then, is the lesson of this book?

A triple one. First, to chastise violence outright, to condemn it as "bad," is an ideological operation par excellence, a mystification which collaborates in rendering invisible the fundamental forms of social violence. It is deeply symptomatic that our Western societies, which display such sensitivity to different

forms of harassment, are at the same time able to mobilise a multitude of mechanisms destined to render
us insensitive to the most brutal forms of violence–often, paradoxically, in the very form of humanitarian
sympathy with the victims.

Second lesson: it is difficult to be really violent, to
perform an act that violently disturbs the basic pa-
rameters of social life. When Bertolt Brecht saw a Japa-
nese mask of an evil demon, he wrote how its swollen
veins and hideous grimaces "all betake / what an ex-
hausting effort it takes / To be evil." The same holds for
violence which has any effect on the system. A standard Hollywood action film is always a lesson in it.
Towards the end of Andrew Davis's *The Fugitive*, the
innocent persecuted doctor (Harrison Ford) confronts
his colleague (Jeroen Krabbé) at a medical convention
and accuses him of falsifying medical data on behalf
of a large pharmaceutical company. At this precise
point, when one would expect a focus on Big Pharma–
corporate capital–as the true culprit, Krabbé inter-
rupts and invites Ford to step outside, and then, outside
the convention hall, engages Ford in a passionate, violent fight: they beat each other till their faces are red
with blood. The scene is telltale in its openly ridiculous character, as if in order to get out of the ideological mess of playing with anti-capitalism, one has to
make a move which renders directly palpable the
cracks in the narrative. The bad guy is transformed
into a vicious, sneering, pathological character, as if psychological depravity (which accompanies the dazzling
spectacle of the fight) somehow replaces and displaces
the anonymous, utterly non-psychological drive of

capital. A much more appropriate gesture would have been to present the corrupted colleague as a psychologically sincere and privately honest doctor who, because of the financial difficulties of the hospital in which he works, was lured into swallowing the bait of the pharmaceutical company . . .

The Fugitive thus provides a clear version of the violent *passage a l'acte* which serves as a lure, the very vehicle of ideological displacement. A step further from this zero level of violence can be found in Paul Schrader's and Martin Scorsese's *Taxi Driver*, in the final outburst of Travis Bickle (Robert De Niro) against the pimps who control the young girl he wants to save (Jodie Foster). Crucial here is the implicit suicidal dimension of this *passage a l'acte*: when Travis prepares for his attack, he practises drawing a gun in front of a mirror: in what is the best-known scene of the film, he addresses his own image in the mirror with the aggressive-condescending "You talkin' to me?" In a textbook illustration of Lacan's notion of the "mirror stage," aggression is here clearly aimed at oneself, at one's own mirror image. This suicidal dimension re-emerges at the end of the slaughter scene when Travis, heavily wounded and leaning against the wall, mimics with the forefinger of his right hand a gun aimed at his bloodstained forehead and mockingly triggers it, as if saying, "The true aim of my outburst was myself." The paradox of Travis is that he perceives *himself* as part of the degenerate dirt of the city life he wants to eradicate, so that, as Brecht put it apropos revolutionary violence in his *The Measure Taken,* he wants to be the last piece of dirt after whose removal the room will be clean.

Mutatis mutandis, the same holds also for large, organised collective violence. The Chinese Cultural Revolution serves as a lesson here: destroying old monuments proved not to be a true negation of the past. Rather it was an impotent *passage a l'acte,* an acting out which bore witness to the failure to get rid of the past. There is a kind of poetic justice in the fact that the final result of Mao's Cultural Revolution is the current unmatched explosion of capitalist dynamics in China. A profound structural homology exists between Maoist permanent self-revolutionising, the permanent struggle against the ossification of state structures, and the inherent dynamics of capitalism. One is tempted to paraphrase Brecht again here: "What is the robbing of a bank compared to the founding of a new bank?" What were the violent and destructive outbursts of a Red Guardist caught in the Cultural Revolution compared to the true Cultural Revolution, the permanent dissolution of all life-forms which capitalist reproduction dictates?

The same, of course, applies to Nazi Germany, where the spectacle of the brutal annihilation of millions should not deceive us. The characterisation of Hitler which would have him as a bad guy, responsible for the deaths of millions but none the less a man with balls who pursued his ends with an iron will, is not only ethically repulsive, it is also simply *wrong*: no, Hitler did not "have the balls" really to change things. All his actions were fundamentally reactions: he acted so that nothing would really change; he acted to prevent the communist threat of a real change. His targeting of the Jews was ultimately an act of displacement in which he avoided the real enemy—the core of capitalist social relations themselves. Hitler staged a spectacle of revolution so that the capitalist order could survive. The irony was that his grand gestures of despising bourgeois self-complacency ultimately enabled this complacency to continue: far from disturbing the much-despised "decadent" bourgeois order, far from awakening the Germans, Nazism was a dream which enabled them to postpone awakening. Germany only really woke up with the defeat of 1945.

If one wants to name an act which was truly daring, for which one truly had to "have balls" to try the impossible, but which was simultaneously an act of horrendous violence, an act which caused suffering beyond comprehension, it was Stalin's forced collectivisation at the end of the 1920s. Yet even this display of ruthless violence culminated in the big purges of 1936–37, which were, again, an impotent *passage a l'acte*:

> This was not a targeting of enemies, but blind rage and panic. It reflected not control of events but a recognition that the regime lacked regularized control mechanisms. It was not policy but the failure of policy. It was a sign of failure to rule with anything but forced.[1]

The very violence inflicted by the communist power on its own members bears witness to the radical self-contradiction of the regime. If at the origins of the regime, there was an "authentic" revolutionary project, incessant purges were necessary not only to erase the traces of the regime's origins, but also as a kind of "return of the repressed," a reminder of the radical negativity at the heart of the regime. The Stalinist purges of

high party echelons relied on this fundamental betrayal:
the accused were effectively guilty insofar as they, as the
members of the new *nomenklatura,* betrayed the Revolution. The Stalinist terror is thus not simply the betrayal of the Revolution, that is, an attempt to erase the
traces of the authentic revolutionary past. It also bears
witness to a kind of "imp of the perverse" which compels the post-revolutionary new order to (re)inscribe its
betrayal of the Revolution within itself, to "reflect" it or
"re-mark" it in the guise of arbitrary arrests and killings which threaten all members of the *nomenklatura.*
As we know from psychoanalysis, the Stalinist confession of guilt conceals the true guilt. It is well known that
Stalin wisely recruited people of lower social origins
into the NKVD. They were thus able to act out their
hatred of the *nomenklatura* by arresting and torturing
high apparatchiks. The inherent tension between the
stability of the rule of the new *nomenklatura* and the
perverted "return of the repressed" in the guise of
the repeated purges of the ranks of the *nomenklatura* is
at the very heart of the Stalinist phenomenon: purges
are the very form in which the betrayed revolutionary
heritage survives and haunts the regime.[2]

In "Murder in the Mews," an early Agatha Christie
story, Poirot investigates the death of Mrs. Allen, found
shot in her apartment on Guy Fawkes night. Although
her death looks like suicide, numerous details indicate
that a murder is more likely and that a clumsy attempt
has been made to make it look as if Mrs. Allen took her
own life. She shared a flat with Miss Plenderleith, who
was away at the time. Soon a cufflink is found at the

murder scene and its owner, Major Eustace, is impli-
cated in the crime. Poirot's solution is one of the best in
Christie's work: it turns round the standard plot of a
murder made to look like suicide. The victim, who
years ago was caught in a scandal in India, where she
also met Eustace, was engaged to marry a Conservative
MP. Knowing that the public exposure of her scandal
would ruin her chances of marriage, Eustace was black-
mailing her. Out of despair, she shot herself. Coming
home immediately after her suicide, Miss Plenderleith–who knew about Eustace's blackmail and hated
him–quickly rearranged details at the scene to make it
appear that the murderer had tried clumsily to present
the death as suicide, so that Eustace would be fully
punished for driving Mrs. Allen to kill herself. The
story thus turns on the question in what direction should
the inconsistencies noted at the scene of the crime be
read. Is it a murder masked as suicide or a suicide
masked as murder? The story works because, instead of
the murder being covered up, as is more usual, its appearance is staged: instead of being concealed, a crime
is created as a lure.

This is precisely what instigators of such violent *passages a l'acte* do. They misconstrue suicide as crime. In
other words, they falsify clues so that a catastrophe
which is a "suicide" (the result of immanent antagonisms) appears as the work of a criminal agent–Jews,
traitors, or reactionaries. This is why, to put it in the
Nietzschean terms which are appropriate here, the ultimate difference between radical-emancipatory politics
and such outbursts of impotent violence is that an authentic political gesture is *active,* it imposes, enforces a

vision, while outbursts of impotent violence are fundamentally *reactive,* a reaction to some disturbing intruder.

Last but not least, the lesson of the intricate relationship between subjective and systemic violence is that violence is not a direct property of some acts, but is distributed between acts and their contexts, between activity and inactivity. The same act can count as violent or non-violent, depending on its context; sometimes a polite smile can be more violent than a brutal outburst. A brief reference to quantum physics might be of some help here; one of the most unsettling notions in quantum physics is that of the Higgs field. Left to their own devices in an environment to which they can pass their energy, all physical systems will eventually assume a state of lowest energy. To put it in another way, the more mass we take from a system, the more we lower its energy, till we reach the vacuum state at which the energy is zero. There are, however, phenomena which compel us to posit the hypothesis that there has to be something (some substance) that *we cannot take away from a given system without RAISING that system's energy*–this "something" is called the Higgs field: once this field *appears* in a vessel that has been pumped empty and whose temperature has been lowered as much as possible, its energy will be further *lowered*. The "something" which thus appears is a something that contains *less* energy than nothing. In short, sometimes zero is not the "cheapest" state of a system, so that, paradoxically, "nothing" costs more than "something." In a crude analogy, the social "nothing" (the stasis of a system, its mere reproduction without any changes) "costs more than something" (a change), that is, it demands a lot of energy, so that the first gesture to provoke a change in the system is to withdraw activity, to do nothing.

José Saramago's novel *Seeing* (the literal translation of the original title is *An Essay on Lucidity*)[3] can effectively be perceived as a mental experiment in Bartlebian politics.[4] It tells the story of the strange events in the unnamed capital city of an unidentified democratic country. When the election day morning is marred by torrential rain, voter turnout is disturbingly low, but the weather breaks by mid-afternoon and the population heads en masse to their voting stations. The government's relief is short lived, however, when vote counting reveals that over 70 per cent of the ballots cast in the capital have been left blank. Baffled by this apparent civic lapse, the government gives the citizenry a chance to make amends just one week later with another election day. The results are worse: now 83 per cent of the ballots are blank. The two major political parties–the ruling party of the right (p.o.t.r.) and their chief adversary, the party of the middle (p.o.t.m.)–are in a panic, while the haplessly marginalised party of the left (p.o.t.l.) produces an analysis claiming that the blank ballots are essentially a vote for their progressive agenda.

Is this an organised conspiracy to overthrow not just the ruling government but the entire democratic system? If so, who is behind it, and how did they manage to organise hundreds of thousands of people into such subversion without being noticed? When asked how they voted, ordinary citizens simply respond that such information is private, and besides, is not leaving the ballot blank their right? Unsure how to respond to a benign protest but certain that an anti-democratic conspiracy exists, the government quickly labels the movement "terrorism, pure and unadulterated" and declares a state of emergency, allowing the government to suspend all constitutional guarantees.

Five hundred citizens are seized at random and disappear into secret interrogation sites, and their status is coded red for secrecy. Their families are informed in Orwellian style not to worry about the lack of information concerning their loved ones, since "in that very silence lay the key that could guarantee their personal safety." When these moves bear no fruit, the right-wing government adopts a series of increasingly drastic steps, from declaring a state of siege and concocting plots to create disorder to withdrawing the police and seat of government from the capital, sealing all the city's entrances and exits, and finally manufacturing its own terrorist ringleader. The city continues to function near-normally throughout, the people parrying each of the government's thrusts in inexplicable unison and with a truly Gandhian level of non-violent resistance.

In his perspicacions review of the novel, Michael Wood noted a Brechtian parallel:

> In a famous poem, written in East Germany in 1953, Brecht quotes a contemporary as saying that the people have lost the trust of the government. Would it not therefore be easier, Brecht slyly asks, to dissolve the people and have the government elect another one? Saramago's novel is a parable of what happens when neither government nor people can be dissolved.[5]

While the parallel holds, the concluding characterisation seems to fall short: the unsettling message of *Seeing* is not so much the indissolubility of both people and government as the compulsive nature of democratic rituals of freedom. What happens is that by abstaining from voting, people effectively dissolve the government–not only in the limited sense of overthrowing the existing government, but more radically. Why is the government thrown into such a panic by the voters' abstention? It is compelled to confront the fact that it exists, that it exerts power, only insofar as it is accepted as such by its subjects–accepted even in the mode of rejection. The voters' abstention goes further than the intra-political negation, the vote of no confidence: it rejects the very frame of decision.

In psychoanalytic terms, the voters' abstention is something like the psychotic *Verwerfung* (foreclosure, rejection/repudiation), which is a more radical move than repression (*Verdrängung*). According to Freud, the repressed is intellectually accepted by the subject, since it is named, and at the same time is negated because the subject refuses to recognise it, refuses to recognise him or herself in it. In contrast to this, foreclosure rejects the term from the symbolic *tout court*. To circumscribe the contours of this radical rejection, one is tempted to evoke Badiou's provocative thesis: "It is better to do nothing than to contribute to the invention of formal ways of rendering visible that which Empire already recognizes as existent."[6] Better to do nothing than to engage in localised acts the ultimate function of which is to make the system run more smoothly (acts such as providing space for the multitude of new subjectivities). The threat today is not passivity, but pseudo-activity, the urge to "be active," to "participate," to mask the nothingness of what goes on. People intervene all the time, "do something"; academics participate in meaningless debates, and so on. The truly difficult thing is to step back, to withdraw. Those in power often prefer even a "critical" participation, a dialogue, to silence–just to engage us in "dialogue," to make sure our ominous passivity is broken. The voters' abstention is thus a true political *act*: it forcefully confronts us with the vacuity of today's democracies.

If one means by violence a radical upheaval of the basic social relations, then, crazy and tasteless as it may sound, the problem with historical monsters who slaughtered millions was that they were not violent enough. Sometimes doing nothing is the most violent thing to do.

NOTES

Introduction

1. Maximilien Robespierre, *Virtue and Terror*, London: Verso, 2007, p. 47.
2. Primo Levi's late book on chemical elements (*The Periodic Table*, New York: Schocken, 1984) should be read against this background of the difficulties–of the fundamental impossibility–to narrativise fully one's condition, to tell one's life story as a consistent narrative: the trauma of the Holocaust prevented it. So, for Levi, the only way to avoid the collapse of his symbolic universe was to find support in some extra-symbolic Real, the Real of classification of chemical elements (and, of course, in his version of the elements, the classification served only as an empty frame: each element was explained in terms of its symbolic associations).
3. "To write poetry after Auschwitz is barbaric." (Theodor W. Adorno, "Cultural Criticism and Society," in Neil Levi and Michael Rothberg (eds.), *The Holocaust: Theoretical Readings*, New Brunswick: Rutgers University Press, 2003, p. 281.)
4. Quoted from Elaine Feinstein, *Anna of all the Russians*, New York: Knopf, 2005, p. 170.
5. Alain Badiou, "Drawing," *lacanian ink* 28 (Autumn 2006), p. 45.
6. See Jean-Paul Sartre, *Existentialism and Humanism*, London: Methuen, 1974.

Chapter 1

1. Lesley Chamberlain, *The Philosophy Steamer*, London: Atlantic Books, 2006, pp. 23–24. To avoid any misunderstanding, let me state clearly that I find this decision to expel the anti-Bolshevik intellectuals totally justified.
2. Ibid., p. 22.

3. Walter Benjamin, "Critique of Violence," in *Selected Writings*, Vol. 1, *1913-1926*, Cambridge, MA: Harvard University Press, 1996.

4. When Palestinians reply to the Israeli demand that they should cease their terrorist attacks with "And what about your occupation of the West Bank?" does Israel also not respond with a version of "Don't change the topic!"?

5. See Etienne Balibar, "La violence: idéalité et cruauté," in *La crainte des masses: politique et philosophie avant et après Marx*, Paris: Editions Galilée, 1997.

6. And therein resides also the limitation of the "ethical committees" which pop up everywhere to counteract the dangers of the unbridled scientific-technological development: with all their good intentions, ethical considerations, etc., they ignore the more basic "systemic" violence.

7. See Olivier Malnuit, "Pourquoi les géants du business se prennent-ils pour Jésus?," *Technikart*, February 2006, pp. 32–37.

8. The same argument applies to the opposition between the "smart" and "non-smart" approach. Outsourcing is the key notion here: by way of outsourcing, you export the (necessary) dark side–disciplined hierarchic labour, ecological pollution . . . –to "non-smart" Third World places (or invisible places in the First World itself). The ultimate liberal communist dream is to export the working class itself to the invisible Third World sweatshops.

9. Peter Sloterdijk, *Zorn und Zeit*, Frankfurt: Suhrkamp, 2006, p. 55.

10. Michael Agger, "Village Idiot: The Case against M. Night Shyamalan," http://www.slate.com/id/2104567.

11. Shane Handler, "M. Night Shyamalan's *The Village*," http://www.glidemagazine.com/articles120.html.

12. David Edelstein, "Village of the Darned: More Pious Hokum from M. Night Shyamalan," http://www.slate.com/id/2104512.

13. One of the more stupid reproaches to the film (not unlike

the same reproach to Hitchcock's *Vertigo*) is that it spoils the suspense by disclosing the secret a mere two-thirds into the film–however, this very knowledge makes the last third all the more interesting. That is to say, the film's last third–more precisely, Ivy's painfully slow progress through the forest–confronts us with a clear enigma (or as some would have put it, narrative inconsistency): why is Ivy afraid of the Creatures, why are the Creatures still presented as a mythic threat when she already knows that Creatures don't exist, that they are a staged fake? In another deleted scene, Ivy, after hearing the ominous (and, as we know, artificially generated) sounds that announce the proximity of the Creatures, cries with desperate intensity: "It is for love that I am here. So I beg you to let me cross!"–why does she do it if she knows there are no Creatures? She knows very well, but . . . there is more reality in the haunting unreal spectres than in direct reality itself.

14. Here, Nicholas Meyer is also right in his Sherlock Holmes pastiche *The Seven-Per-Cent Solution*. Within the diegetic space of Sherlock Holmes stories, Moriarty, the arch-criminal–"Napoleon of crime"–and Holmes's ultimate opponent, is clearly a fantasy of Holmes himself, his double, his Dark Half: in the opening pages of Meyer's novel, Watson is visited by Moriarty, a humble mathematics professor, who complains to Watson that Holmes is obsessed with the idée fixe that he is the master criminal; to cure Holmes, Watson lures him to Vienna, to Freud's house.

15. Available online at http://www.impactservices.net.au/movies/childrenofmen.htm.

16. Friedrich Nietzsche, *Thus Spake Zarathustra,* New York: Prometheus, 1993, p. 41.

17. John Gray, *Straw Dogs,* London: Granta, 2003, p. 161.

18. Available online at http://www.masturbate-a-thon.com.

19. Alain Badiou, *Logiques des mondes,* Paris: Editions du Seuil, 2006.

20. Ibid.

21. For the concept of the Master-Signifier, see Jacques Lacan, *The Other Side of Psychoanalysis,* New York: Norton, 2006.

22. Badiou, *Logiques des mondes,* p. 443.

23. For example, Michel Houellebecq, *The Possibility of an Island,* New York: Knopf, 2006.

24. Nicholas Sabloff, "Of Filth and Frozen Dinners," *Common Review,* Winter 2007, p. 50.

25. Ibid., p. 51.

26. Bertolt Brecht, "Verhoer des Guten," in *Werke,* Vol. 18, *Prosa 3,* Frankfurt am Main: Suhrkamp Verlag, 1995, pp. 502–503 (author's translation).

Chapter 2

1. For the notion of bio-politics, see Giorgio Agamben, *Homo sacer,* Stanford: Stanford University Press, 1998; for the notion of post-politics, see Jacques Rancière, *Disagreement,* Minneapolis: University of Minnesota Press, 1998.

2. See also Agamben, *Homo sacer.*

3. Sam Harris, *The End of Faith,* New York: Norton, 2005, p. 199.

4. Ibid., pp. 192–93.

5. Ibid., p. 197.

6. Epigraph of "Living Room Dialogues on the Middle East," quoted from Wendy Brown, *Regulating Aversion: Tolerance in the Age of Identity and Empire,* Princeton: Princeton University Press, 2006, p. 1.

7. David Remnick, *Lenin's Tomb,* New York: Random House, 1993, p. 11.

8. This is why anyone interested in the topic of evil should look at Claudia Koonz's *The Nazi Conscience* (Cambridge, MA: Belknap Press, 2003), a detailed report on the Nazi ethical discourse which provided the rationale for their crimes.

9. Theodor W. Adorno and Walter Benjamin, *The Complete*

Correspondence 1928–1940, Cambridge, MA: Harvard University Press, 1999, p. 252.

10. Martin Amis, "All that Survives Is Love," *The Times*, 1 June 2006, pp. 4–5.

11. Immanuel Kant, "The Conflict of Faculties," in *Political Writings*, Cambridge: Cambridge University Press, 1991, p. 182.

12. Sloterdijk, *Zorn und Zeit*, p. 134.

13. Available online at http://thinkexist.com/quotes/neil _gaiman.

14. Peter Sloterdijk, "Warten auf den Islam," *Focus*, October 2006, p. 84.

15. The idea propagated by Habermas (see Jürgen Habermas, *The Theory of Communicative Action*, 2 vols., New York: Beacon Press, 1985), but also not strange to a certain Lacan (see Jacques Lacan, "The Function and Field of Speech and Language in Psychoanalysis," in *Ecrits*, New York: Norton, 2006).

16. Jean-Marie Muller, "Non-Violence in Education," http://portal.unesco.org/education/en/file_download.php/fa99ea234f4accb0ad43040e1d60809cmuller_en.pdf.

17. Ibid.

18. See Clément Rosset, *Le réel: traité de l'idiotie*, Paris: Editions de Minuit, 2004, pp. 112–14.

19. For the concept of the four discourses, see Lacan, *The Other Side of Psychoanalysis*.

20. Muller, "Non-Violence in Education."

21. Simone Weil, *Œuvres complètes VI: Cahiers*, Vol. 2, *September 1941–February 1942*, Paris: Gallimard, 1997, p. 74.

22. Simone Weil, *Œuvres complètes VI: Cahiers*, Vol. 1, *1933–September 1941*, Paris: Gallimard, 1994, p. 325.

23. G. K. Chesterton, "A Defence of Detective Stories," in H. Haycraft (ed.), *The Art of the Mystery Story*, New York: Universal Library, 1946, p. 6.

24. Mark Wrathall, *How to Read Heidegger*, London: Granta, 2005, pp. 94–95.

25. Martin Heidegger, *Introduction to Metaphysics,* New Haven: Yale University Press, 2000, pp. 115–28.

26. The topic of this violence was developed by both Walter Benjamin and Carl Schmitt: Benjamin, "Critique of Violence"; Carl Schmitt, *The Concept of the Political,* Chicago: University of Chicago Press, 1996.

27. See Rosset, *Le réel,* pp. 22–23.

28. Heidegger, *Introduction to Metaphysics,* p. 102.

29. Simone de Beauvoir, *America Day by Day,* quoted from Stella Sandford, *How to Read Beauvoir,* London: Granta, 2006, p. 42.

30. Ibid., p. 49.

Chapter 3

1. Here also, as in the case of the relationship between the Los Angeles riots (after videos were shown of the police beating Rodney King) and Hollywood films, what effectively happened had already been felt and seen a decade earlier–recall *La haine* (Mathieu Kassovitz, 1995), the black-and-white film about the French suburban intifada, portraying senseless juvenile violence, police brutality, and social exclusion in the Paris suburbs. There is no potential in these outbursts for the rise of a properly political agent–all one can hope is that they will survive in some kind of cultural registration, like the rise of a new suburban punk culture.

2. See Roman Jakobson, "Closing Statement: Linguistics and Poetics," in T. A. Sebeok (ed.), *Style in Language,* New York: Wiley, 1960, pp. 350–77.

3. Alain Badiou, "The Caesura of Nihilism," lecture delivered at the University of Essex, 10 September 2003.

4. Gray, *Straw Dogs,* p. 19.

5. For the concept of the "university discourse," see Lacan, *The Other Side of Psychoanalysis.*

6. See Donald Davidson, *Essays on Actions and Events,* Oxford: Oxford University Press, 1980.

7. Jean-Pierre Dupuy, *Avions-nous oublié le mal? Penser la politique après le 11 septembre*, Paris: Bayard, 2002.

8. Quoted in Bradley K. Martin, *Under the Loving Care of the Fatherly Leader*, New York: Thomas Dunne, 2004, p. 85.

9. Was not, even before Satan's famous "Evil, be thou my Good" from Milton's *Paradise Lost*, the formula of the diabolical evil provided already by Shakespeare, in whose *Titus Andronicus* the unrepentant Aaron's final words are "If one good deed in all my life I did, / I do repent it from my very soul"?

10. The most famous example is Robert Axelrod, *The Evolution of Cooperation*, New York: Basic Books, 1984.

11. Dupuy is wrong in his characterisation of the Lacanian psychoanalysis as part of the ongoing "mechanisation of the mind"–psychoanalysis, on the contrary, reintroduces notions of evil and responsibility into our ethical vocabulary; "death drive" is the name for what disturbs the homeostatic mechanism of rational pleasure-seeking, the weird reversal where I sabotage my own interests. If this is the true evil, then not only today's secular pragmatic ethical theories, but even the "mechanisation of the mind" in cognitive sciences, are to be conceived not as in themselves "evil," but as a defence against evil.

12. Lacan, *Ecrits*, pp. 689–98.

13. See Dupuy, *Avions-nous oublié le mal?*

14. John Rawls, *A Theory of Justice*, Cambridge, MA: Harvard University Press, 1971 (revised edition 1999).

15. In a more morbid version, the witch tells him: "I will do to you whatever you want, but I warn you, I will do it to your neighbour twice!" The peasant, with a cunning smile, asks her: "Take one of my eyes!"

16. See Friedrich Hayek, *The Road to Serfdom*, Chicago: University of Chicago Press, 1994.

17. See Alenka Zupancic, *The Shortest Shadow*, Cambridge, MA: MIT Press, 2006.

18. Is it possible to envy oneself, not just another subject? About subjects who, unable to endure their happiness or luck, obstinately sabotage themselves, one can sometimes effectively say, in crudely Freudian terms, that their superego envies the success of their ego. The split between what Lacan calls the "subject of enunciated" (the way the I, the speaking subject, represents itself in its speech) and the "subject of enunciation" (the speaking I itself) is brought to extreme here: the subject becomes his own Other, occupying a position from which he envies himself.

19. Jean-Jacques Rousseau, *Rousseau, Judge of Jean-Jacques: Dialogues,* Hanover, NH: Dartmouth College Press, 1990, p. 63 (italics added).

20. See Jean-Pierre Dupuy, *Petite metaphysique des tsunamis,* Paris: Editions du Seuil, 2005, p. 68.

21. However, it had already happened in the U.S.: on film, of course: the *Escape from . . .* series (*Escape from New York, Escape from Los Angeles*), in which a U.S. megalopolis is cut off from the domain of public order and criminal gangs take over. More interesting in this respect is David Koepp's *The Trigger Effect* from 1996, in which, when the power goes out in the big city, society starts to break down; the film plays imaginatively with race relations and our prejudicial attitudes toward strangers–as the publicity for the film put it: "When nothing works, anything goes." Even further behind is lurking the aura of New Orleans as the city of vampires, living dead, and voodoo, where some dark spiritual force is always threatening to rip the social fabric. So, again, as with 9/11, the surprise was not just a surprise: what happened was not that the self-enclosed ivory tower of U.S. life was shattered by the intrusion of the Third World reality of social chaos, violence, and hunger, but on the contrary, that (what was hitherto perceived as) something which is not part of our reality, something of which we were only aware as a

fictional presence on TV and theatre screens, brutally entered our reality.

22. For the concept of the "subject supposed to believe," see Chapter 3 of Slavoj Žižek, *The Plague of Fantasies,* London: Verso, 1997.

23. See Jim Dwyer and Christopher Drew, "Fear Exceeded Crime's Reality in New Orleans," *New York Times,* 29 September 2005.

Chapter 4

1. See Immanuel Kant, "The Antinomy of Pure Reason," in *Critique of Pure Reason: The Transcendental Dialectic,* London: Palgrave, 2003, Book II, Chapter 2.

2. This total responsibility of the woman for the sexual act has been legally upheld in Iran, where, on 3 January 2006, a nineteen-year-old girl was sentenced to death by hanging after admitting having stabbed to death one of three men who tried to rape her. Here is the paradox: if she had elected not to defend herself, and allowed the men to rape her, she would have been subjected to 100 lashes under the Iranian laws on chastity; if she had been married at the time of the rape, she would possibly have been found guilty of adultery and sentenced to death by stoning. So whatever happens, the responsibility is hers alone.

3. However, there is another, more ominous, reading of this lack of responsibility of men: is such an ability to perform the sexual act anytime, anywhere not a feminine fantasy? Recall the ridiculous Taliban prohibition, when they were still in power in Afghanistan, of metal heels for women–as if even if women are entirely covered with cloth, the clanging sound of their heels would still provoke men. Does this, again, not presuppose a totally eroticised image of man who can be aroused even by so innocent a sound if it signals a woman's presence? The other side of the Western tolerance for sexually provocative behaviour in women would then have been that in our permissive

societies, men are less and less interested in sexual intercourse and consider it more a duty than a pleasure.

4. This, of course, in no way justifies Irving, who was invited to Austria by a far-right party and knew that he would be arrested there.

5. And insofar as any probing into the number of the dead is also disqualified, one can imagine the ultimate obscenity debating at what level to put the "tolerable" number of the dead, which would strangely echo the debate about the amount of alcohol that should be permitted in the driver's blood: should it be 5.5 million or are you still a respected historian rather than a Holocaust-revisionist if you claim that "merely" 5.3 million Jews were killed?

6. Iranian President Mahmoud Ahmadinejad at the Islamic summit in Mecca on 8 December 2005, as reported by Associated Press.

7. See Alain Badiou and Cécile Winter, *Circonstances,* Vol. 3, *Portées du mot 'Juif',* Paris: Leo Scheer, 2005.

8. See Oriana Fallaci, *The Rage and the Pride,* New York: Rizzoli, 2002; *The Force of Reason,* New York: Rizzoli, 2006.

9. Menachem Begin, *The Revolt,* New York: Dell, 1977, pp. 100–101.

10. The letter appeared as a full-page advertisement on page 42 of the 14 May 1947 edition of the *New York Post.* The full text is available online at http://scotland.indymedia.org/newswire/display/3510/index.php.

11. Quoted from *Time* magazine, 24 July 2006.

12. Simon Wiesenthal, *Justice Not Vengeance,* London: Mandarin, 1989, p. 266.

13. Ibid., p. 265.

14. Norman Davies, *Europe At War,* London: Macmillan, 2006, p. 346.

15. Alain Badiou, "The Question of Democracy," *lacanian ink* 28 (Autumn 2006), p. 59.

16. Similarly, one should praise Ehud Barak's response to

Gideon Levy for *Ha'aretz*, when Barak was asked what he would have done if he had been born a Palestinian: "I would have joined a terrorist organization." (Available online at http://www.monabaker.com/quotes.htm.)

17. See Karl Marx, "Class Struggles in France," *Collected Works*, Vol. 10, London: Lawrence and Wishart, 1978, p. 95.

18. Quoted from Edward T. Oakes, "Darwin's Graveyards," *Books & Culture*, November/December 2006, p. 36.

19. André Glucksmann, *Dostoievski à Manhattan*, Paris: Robert Laffont, 2002.

20. There is a similar version in Sufi Islam: "O Lord, if I worship you out of fear of Hell, burn me in Hell. If I worship you in the hope of Paradise, forbid it to me. And if I worship you for your own sake, do not deprive me of your eternal beauty" (Rabi'a al-'Adawiyya of Basra, 713–801).

Chapter 5

1. I rely here extensively on Brown, *Regulating Aversion*.

2. See Samuel Huntington, *The Clash of Civilizations*, New York: Simon and Schuster, 1998.

3. See Francis Fukuyama, *The End of History and the Last Man*, New York: Free Press, 2006 (reprint edition).

4. This, incidentally, gives a new twist to the infamous formula attributed to Hermann Goering, "When I hear the word 'culture,' I reach for my revolver"–but not, of course, when I hear the word "civilisation."

5. René Descartes, *Discourse on Method*, South Bend, IN: University of Notre Dame Press, 1994, p. 33.

6. Quoted from Ziauddin Sardar and Merryl Wyn Davies, *The No-Nonsense Guide to Islam*, London: New Internationalist/Verso, 2004, p. 77.

7. See Claude Lefort, *The Political Forms of Modern Society: Bureaucracy, Democracy, Totalitarianism*, Cambridge, MA: MIT Press, 1986; Jacques Rancière, *Hatred of Democracy*, London: Verso, 2007.

8. See Marx, "Class Struggles in France," p. 95.

9. Moustapha Safouan, "Why Are the Arabs Not Free? The Politics of Writing" (unpublished manuscript).

10. Perhaps this feature accounts for another weird phenomenon: in (almost) all American hotels housed in buildings of more than twelve floors, there is no 13th floor (to avoid bad luck, of course), i.e., one jumps directly from the 12th floor to the 14th. For a European, such a procedure is meaningless: who are we trying to fool? As if God doesn't know that what we designated as the 14th floor is really the 13th floor? Americans can play this game precisely because their God is just a prolongation of our individual egos, not perceived as a true ground of being.

11. George Orwell, *The Road to Wigan Pier*, London: Gollancz, 1937.

12. Although even here the benevolent Welfare State endeavours to balance the annoyance of the bad-smelling Neighbour with health concerns: a couple of years ago, the Dutch health ministry advised citizens to break wind at least fifteen times per day in order to avoid unhealthy tensions and pressures in the body.

13. "For to every one who has will more be given, and he will have abundance; but from him who has not, even what he has will be taken away" (Matthew 25:29).

14. For a more detailed elaboration of this topic, see Chapter 3 of Slavoj Žižek, *The Metastases of Enjoyment*, London: Verso, 1995.

15. Christopher Hitchens, "Prison Mutiny," http://www.slate .com/id/2099888/.

Chapter 6

1. This "divine" dimension reverberates in the shower-murder of Marion, a scene in which violence erupts out of nowhere.

2. Walter Benjamin, "Theses on the Philosophy of History," Thesis IX, in *Illuminations*, New York: Schocken Books, 1968.

3. As to diverse modalities of divine violence, see Terry Eagleton, *Sweet Violence: The Idea of the Tragic,* Oxford: Blackwell, 2002.

4. One should recall here that the story of Job also plays a crucial role in Islam, for which Job is the epitome of a pure believer.

5. See Chapter 3 in Raymond Bellour, *The Analysis of Film,* Bloomington: Indiana University Press, 2000.

6. Available online at www.cse.dmu.ac.uk/~mward/gkc/books/oracle.html.

7. Sloterdijk's entire development of "spheres" is based on this shift of accent: "spheres" are maternal wombs reconstructed at an expanded level, from houses to language itself as the "house of being."

8. Sloterdijk proposes in *Zorn und Zeit* an interesting critical reading of Lacan: Freud's central weakness is his exclusive focus on *eros,* which makes him unable to account for thymotic struggles (the death drive, invented to do this job, miserably fails); to counteract Freud's weakness, Lacan "thymotises" *eros* itself (reinterpreting Freud through Hegel–Kojève: desire is always also a desire for recognition, its fulfilment is the recognition of desire, etc.), but thus misses the specificity of erotics.

9. Sloterdijk, *Zorn und Zeit,* p. 107. The irony is that in this work Sloterdijk regularly resorts to the term *Linksfaschismus* made famous by his arch-opponent in Germany, Jürgen Habermas, who used it back in 1968 to denounce violent student protesters who wanted to replace debate with more "direct action." Perhaps this detail tells us more than may at first appear, since Sloterdijk's conclusion, his "positive programme," is not so different from Habermas's, in spite of their public antagonism.

10. W. G. Sebald, *On the Natural History of Destruction,* London: Penguin, 2003, pp. 160–62.

11. Against this background, one should also reject the standard formula of justifying one's violent acts of revenge

with the excuse often used by the Israelis about Palestinians, that they "have" to bomb them: "I will forgive you your crimes, but I will never forgive you the fact that you make me do to you the violent acts I have no choice but to do"–one can well imagine Hitler or Himmler saying the same thing to Jews!

12. Available online at http://www.kafka-franz.com/KAFKA-letter.htm.

13. Is this not why Nietzsche himself descended into madness? Do the last months preceding his final breakdown not stand under the sign of an ambiguous envy at the enigma of Christ? Recall how, in this difficult period, he often signed his name "Christ."

14. Jacques Lacan, *The Ethics of Psychoanalysis*, London: Routledge, 1992, Chapters 19–21.

15. See Jacques Lacan, "Kant with Sade," in *Ecrits*, pp. 645–68.

16. Friedrich Engels, "Introduction" to Karl Marx, *The Civil War in France*, in *Marx/Engels/Lenin on Historical Materialism*, New York: International Publishers, 1974, p. 242.

17. Benjamin, "Critique of Violence," pp. 249–51. The German word *Gewalt* means both "violence" and "authority" or "established power." (A similar link can be found in the English phrase "to enforce the law," which suggests that it is impossible to think about the law without referring to a certain violence, both at the origin, when the law is first created, and repeatedly, when the law is "applied.")

18. See Eric Santner, *On the Psychotheology of Everyday Life*, Chicago: University of Chicago Press, 2001.

19. Benjamin, "Critique of Violence," p. 252.

20. Quoted in Simon Schama, *Citizens*, New York: Viking, 1989, pp. 706–707.

21. Robespierre, *Virtue and Terror*, p. 59.

22. Ibid., p. 129.

23. Quoted from Jon Lee Anderson, *Che Guevara: A Revolutionary Life*, New York: Grove Press, 1997, p. 636.

24. Available online at http://www.marxists.org/archive/ guevara/1967/04/16.htm.

25. Quoted from Peter McLaren, *Che Guevara, Paulo Freire, and the Pedagogy of Revolution,* Oxford: Rowman & Littlefield, 2000, p. 27.

26. Søren Kierkegaard, *Works of Love,* New York: Harper & Row, 1962, p. 114.

Epilogue

1. J. Arch Getty and Oleg V. Naumov, *The Road to Terror. Stalin and the Self-Destruction of the Bolsheviks, 1932–39,* New Haven and London: Yale University Press, 1999, p. 14.

2. The standard condemnation of Stalin comprises two propositions: (1) he was a cynic who knew very well how things stood (that the accused at the show trials were really innocent, etc.); (2) he knew what he was doing, i.e., he did have full control over the events. Documents from the newly accessible archives rather point to the opposite sense: Stalin basically *did* believe (in the official ideology, in his role as an honest leader, in the guilt of the accused, etc.), and he did *not* really control the events (the actual results of his own measures and interventions often shocked him). See Lars T. Lih's outstanding "Introduction" to Lars T. Lih, Oleg V. Naumov, and Oleg V. Khlevniuk (eds.), *Stalin's Letters to Molotov,* New Haven: Yale University Press, 1995, pp. 60–64; Lih proposed a distressing conclusion: "The people of the Soviet Union would probably have been better off if Stalin had been more cynical than he was" (p. 48).

3. José Saramago, *Seeing,* New York: Harcourt, 2006.

4. "Bartlebian," of course, refers to Herman Melville's Bartleby, an uncannily passive New York clerk who answers every demand of his boss to do something with "I would prefer not to."

5. Michael Wood, "The Election With No Results," http://

www.slate.com/id/2139519/. There is another Brechtian dimension in the novel noted by Wood, who also says about Saramago's books: "These are novels, not essays. But they do glance at the essay form. The people in these works don't have names, only roles: the minister of justice, the doctor's wife, the policeman, the officer of the polling station, and so on. Their exchanges of speech are marked only by commas and upper-case letters; no quotation marks, no line spacing. Both characters and dialogue are clustered into social forms, as if a whole culture were talking and acting through its most identifiable representatives." Is this not strictly homologous to Brecht's austere "learning plays" in which people also do not have names, only roles (capitalist, worker, revolutionary, policeman), so that it is as if "a whole culture [or rather, ideology] were talking and acting through its most identifiable representatives"?

6. Alain Badiou, "Fifteen Theses on Contemporary Art," *lacanian ink* 23 (Spring 2004), p. 119.

BIBLIOGRAPHY

Adorno, Theodor W. "Cultural Criticism and Society." In Neil Levi and Michael Rothberg (eds.), *The Holocaust: Theoretical Readings*. New Brunswick: Rutgers University Press, 2003.

Adorno, Theodor W., and Walter Benjamin. *The Complete Correspondence 1928-1940*. Cambridge, MA: Harvard University Press, 1999.

Agamben, Giorgio. *Homo sacer*. Stanford: Stanford University Press, 1998.

Anderson, Jon Lee. *Che Guevara: A Revolutionary Life*. New York: Grove Press, 1997.

Axelrod, Robert. *The Evolution of Cooperation*. New York: Basic Books, 1984.

Badiou, Alain. "Drawing." *lacanian ink* 28 (Autumn 2006), pp. 43–47.

——. "Fifteen Theses on Contemporary Art." *lacanian ink* 23 (Spring 2004), pp. 100–119.

——. *Logiques des mondes*. Paris: Editions du Seuil, 2006.

——. "The Question of Democracy." *lacanian ink* 28 (Autumn 2006), pp. 51–67.

Badiou, Alain, and Cécile Winter. *Circonstances*, Vol. 3, *Portées du mot "Juif."* Paris: Leo Scheer, 2005.

Balibar, Etienne. *La crainte des masses: politique et philosophie avant et après Marx*. Paris: Editions Galilée, 1997.

Begin, Menachem. *The Revolt*. New York: Dell, 1977.

Bellour, Raymond. *The Analysis of Film*. Bloomington: Indiana University Press, 2000.

Benjamin, Walter. "Critique of Violence." In *Selected Writings*, Vol. 1, *1913-1926*. Cambridge, MA: Harvard University Press, 1996, pp. 249–51.

——. *Illuminations*. New York: Schocken Books, 1968.

Brecht, Bertolt. "Verhoer des Guten." In *Werke*, Vol. 18, Prosa 3. Frankfurt am Main: Suhrkamp Verlag, 1995, pp. 502–503.

Brown, Wendy. *Regulating Aversion: Tolerance in the Age of Identity and Empire.* Princeton: Princeton University Press, 2006.

Chamberlain, Lesley. *The Philosophy Steamer.* London: Atlantic Books, 2006.

Chesterton, G. K. "A Defence of Detective Stories." In H. Haycraft (ed.), *The Art of the Mystery Story.* New York: Universal Library, 1946, pp. 3–6.

Davidson, Donald. *Essays on Actions and Events.* Oxford: Oxford University Press, 1980.

Davies, Norman. *Europe At War.* London: Macmillan, 2006.

Descartes, René. *Discourse on Method.* South Bend, IN: University of Notre Dame Press, 1994.

Dupuy, Jean-Pierre. *Avions-nous oublié le mal? Penser la politique après le 11 septembre.* Paris: Bayard, 2002.

——. *Petite metaphysique des tsunamis.* Paris: Editions du Seuil, 2005.

Eagleton, Terry. *Sweet Violence: The Idea of the Tragic.* Oxford: Blackwell, 2002.

Engels, Friedrich. "Introduction" to Karl Marx, *The Civil War in France.* In *Marx/Engels/Lenin on Historical Materialism.* New York: International Publishers, 1974.

Fallaci, Oriana. *The Force of Reason.* New York: Rizzoli, 2006.

——. *The Rage and the Pride.* New York: Rizzoli, 2002.

Feinstein, Elaine. *Anna of all the Russians.* New York: Knopf, 2005.

Fukuyama, Francis. *The End of History and the Last Man.* New York: Free Press, 2006 (reprint edition).

Getty, J. Arch, and Oleg V. Naumov. *The Road to Terror. Stalin and the Self-Destruction of the Bolsheviks, 1932–39.* New Haven and London: Yale University Press, 1999.

Glucksmann, André. *Dostoievski à Manhattan.* Paris: Robert Laffont, 2002.

Gray, John. *Straw Dogs.* London: Granta, 2003.

Habermas, Jürgen. *The Theory of Communicative Action.* 2 vols. New York: Beacon Press, 1985.

Harris, Sam. *The End of Faith*. New York: Norton, 2005.

Hayek, Friedrich. *The Road to Serfdom*. Chicago: University of Chicago Press, 1994.

Heidegger, Martin. *Introduction to Metaphysics*. New Haven: Yale University Press, 2000.

Houellebecq, Michel. *The Possibility of an Island*. New York: Knopf, 2006.

Huntington, Samuel. *The Clash of Civilizations*. New York: Simon and Schuster, 1998.

Jakobson, Roman. "Closing Statement: Linguistics and Poetics." In T. A. Sebeok (ed.), *Style in Language*. New York: Wiley, 1960, pp. 350–77.

Kant, Immanuel. *Critique of Pure Reason: The Transcendental Dialectic*. London: Palgrave, 2003.

———. *Political Writings*. Cambridge: Cambridge University Press, 1991.

Kierkegaard, Søren. *Works of Love*. New York: Harper & Row, 1962.

Koonz, Claudia. *The Nazi Conscience*. Cambridge, MA: Belknap Press, 2003.

Lacan, Jacques. *Ecrits*. New York: Norton, 2006.

———. *The Ethics of Psychoanalysis*. London: Routledge, 1992.

———. *The Other Side of Psychoanalysis*. New York: Norton, 2006.

Lefort, Claude. *The Political Forms of Modern Society: Bureaucracy, Democracy, Totalitarianism*. Cambridge, MA: MIT Press, 1986.

Levi, Primo. *The Periodic Table*. New York: Schocken, 1995.

Lih, Lars T., Oleg V. Naumov, and Oleg V. Khlevniuk (eds.). *Stalin's Letters to Molotov*. New Haven: Yale University Press, 1995.

Malnuit, Olivier. "Pourquoi les géants du business se prennent-ils pour Jésus?" *Technikart*, February 2006, pp. 32–37.

Martin, Bradley K. *Under the Loving Care of the Fatherly Leader*. New York: Thomas Dunne, 2004.

Marx, Karl. *Collected Works*. Vol. 10. London: Lawrence and Wishart, 1978.

McLaren, Peter. *Che Guevara, Paulo Freire, and the Pedagogy of Revolution*. Oxford: Rowman & Littlefield, 2000.

Nietzsche, Friedrich. *Thus Spake Zarathustra*. New York: Prometheus, 1993.

Oakes, Edward T. "Darwin's Graveyards." *Books & Culture*, November/December 2006, pp. 35–38.

Orwell, George. *The Road to Wigan Pier*. London: Gollancz, 1937.

Rancière, Jacques. *Disagreement*. Minneapolis: University of Minnesota Press, 1998.

——. *Hatred of Democracy*. London: Verso, 2007.

Rawls, John. *A Theory of Justice*. Cambridge, MA: Harvard University Press, 1971 (revised edition 1999).

Remnick, David. *Lenin's Tomb*. New York: Random House, 1993.

Robespierre, Maximilien. *Virtue and Terror*. London: Verso, 2007.

Rosset, Clément. *Le réel: traité de l'idiotie*. Paris: Editions de Minuit, 2004.

Rousseau, Jean-Jacques. *Rousseau, Judge of Jean-Jacques: Dialogues*. Hanover, NH: Dartmouth College Press, 1990.

Sabloff, Nicholas. "Of Filth and Frozen Dinners." *Common Review*, Winter 2007, pp. 50–52.

Sandford, Stella. *How to Read Beauvoir*. London: Granta, 2006.

Santner, Eric. *On the Psychotheology of Everyday Life*. Chicago: University of Chicago Press, 2001.

Saramago, José. *Seeing*. New York: Harcourt, 2006.

Sardar, Ziauddin, and Merryl Wyn Davies. *The No-Nonsense Guide to Islam*. London: New Internationalist/Verso, 2004.

Sartre, Jean-Paul. *Existentialism and Humanism*. London: Methuen, 1974.

Schama, Simon. *Citizens*. New York: Viking, 1989.

Schmitt, Carl. *The Concept of the Political*. Chicago: University of Chicago Press, 1996.

Sebald, W. G. *On the Natural History of Destruction*. London: Penguin, 2003.

Sloterdijk, Peter. *Zorn und Zeit*. Frankfurt: Suhrkamp, 2006.

Weil, Simone. *Œuvres complètes VI: Cahiers*. Vol. 1, *1933–September 1941*. Paris: Gallimard, 1994; Vol. 2, *September 1941–February 1942*. Paris: Gallimard, 1997.

Wiesenthal, Simon. *Justice Not Vengeance*. London: Mandarin, 1989.

Wrathall, Mark. *How to Read Heidegger*. London: Granta, 2005.

Žižek, Slavoj. *The Metastases of Enjoyment*. London: Verso, 1995.

——. *The Plague of Fantasies*. London: Verso, 1997.

Zupancic, Alenka. *The Shortest Shadow*. Cambridge, MA: MIT Press, 2006.

BIBLIOGRAPHY

INDEX